C000165327

HERTFORD
& BEDFORDSHIRE
MURDERS

Other counties in this series include:

Berkshire   Sussex
Devon   Warwickshire
Northamptonshire Yorkshire
Surrey

HERTFORDSHIRE & BEDFORDSHIRE MURDERS

Paul Harrison

COUNTRYSIDE BOOKS
NEWBURY, BERKSHIRE

First Published 1993
© Paul Harrison 1993

All rights reserved
No reproduction permitted without
the prior permission of the publishers:

COUNTRYSIDE BOOKS
3 Catherine Road
Newbury, Berkshire

ISBN 1 85306 263 4

*Dedicated to the memory
of my dear brother,
John Scott Harrison
('Lest we forget')*

Produced through MRM Associates Ltd, Reading
Typeset by Paragon Typesetters, Queensferry
Printed in England

Contents

WITH MALICE
AFORETHOUGHT

THE British policing system, in a very rudimentary form, can be traced back as far as 1195 when the Knights of Richard the Lionheart were entrusted to keep each county's peace, but the office of magistrate was first mentioned in a statute of 1324 when it was decreed, 'In every county there shall be assigned a good and lawful man to keep the peace'. In 1361 the Justice of the Peace Act was formulated and passed in order to develop strict guidelines for such officials, who received their authority from the Crown. These responsibilities were in turn delegated to subordinates who were known as the parish constables. Eventually, with these officers carrying out the duties for the magistrate, the latter were provided and entrusted with further powers within their respective parish boundaries.

The magistrate tended to be selected from the more affluent members of each society, those with sufficient funds to delegate responsibility for a miserly payment, and the unfortunate constables of each parish found their duties and responsibilities anything but enjoyable. The constable was elected via a local ballot, and it was a totally voluntary role in as much as there was no official payment for carrying out such duties. However, in many cases when a more wealthy member of the parish was elected to the position he would offer it to another for a small payment. With the lower end of the social ladder taking up the position of parish constable

Senior officers of Hertford Borough Police around 1880.
(Courtesy Geoff Harris)

Watford's policemen in about 1880. (Courtesy Geoff Harris)

it is no surprise to find that these poor souls were generally blessed with the minimum amount of commonsense, and they were easily confused and misguided. The role also meant that any prisoners would be held in the constable's own home, no provision being made for this, and it generally meant that the officer would have to sit up and personally guard his prisoner all night, until he could be tried and ultimately jailed.

The early days of policing in England and Wales can be best described as farcical, with naive beliefs and old wives' tales being generally accepted as truth. One such belief was that the body of a murder victim would bleed if the killer was forced to touch the corpse. A reference to this can be found in the Hertfordshire records of 1631, where it is recorded that the body of a murdered woman was exhumed some 30 days after her burial. The alleged killer was brought before the corpse and made to touch it, and upon doing so various changes are said to have taken place. The deceased opened and closed one eyelid several times, seemingly drew breath with its chest rising and falling several times, and then finally the ring finger of the left hand dripped blood onto the floor. This 'evidence' was related in court by a minister of the parish in which the crime occurred. The Chief Justice was extremely sceptical and requested further corroboration of the facts, so a second minister from an adjoining parish duly came forward and related an identical story, added to which he confirmed that his colleague was a perfectly sane man, not prone to exaggeration! The unfortunate suspect was duly executed on this evidence.

Footpads, or highwaymen as they are more popularly known, have played a major role in the criminal history of both counties. The area's most celebrated highway robbers have included Thomas Dun, whose activities are recorded in full elsewhere in this work, and the Wicked Lady of Markyate, but there were countless others who roamed the highways in search of ill-gotten gains. Henry Powel was a native of London, who had grown up in an affluent environment but had elected to mix with a more unsavoury group who taught him the habits of the underworld. On 15th October 1715 he ventured north, to South Mimms, Hertfordshire where he carried out a number of highway robberies. He stopped one Sarah Maddocks and stole two shillings and sixpence from her, but before he could make good his escape a number of gentlemen caught him and he was eventually brought before a magistrate. Powel was found guilty of highway robbery and sentenced to death; this was carried out at the famous London prison of Newgate. Generally, criminals were executed within the county where they were caught committing the crime but on this occasion Powel was wanted for so many other similar offences in London that it was decided to switch the trial and judgement to the nation's capital.

The Municipal Corporations Act of 1835 empowered borough councils to form a 'Watch Committee' who would be responsible for providing sufficient manpower to create a respectable policing system within their boundaries. The Watch Committee of Bedford elected seven members of their population to serve as police officers, their duties commencing on 16th January 1836. The first appointed Chief Constable was William Coombes, who received a salary of ten shillings and sixpence, precisely the sum paid to each constable, albeit he did have a few extra perks with his position. The Hertford Borough Police were formed during the same period, and this force was quickly followed by the St Albans Borough Police in July 1836. Thus 'official' policing of the two counties began.

The police forces of Hertfordshire and Bedfordshire as we now know them were formed within twelve months of each other. Bedfordshire Constabulary was founded in March 1840, the first Chief Constable being Captain Edward M

Boultbee who was to find some 46 officers for the new force; six were made superintendents (through social status rather than policing experience), the rest were constables. In April 1841 Hertfordshire Constabulary was formed, and Chief Constable Colonel A Robertson employed some 70 officers to police 120,000 inhabitants within the county. The force had four superintendents, six inspectors and 60 constables. The Hertford and St Albans Borough police forces remained autonomous of the County Constabulary until 1889 when the Hertford Borough amalgamated; the St Albans Borough did not do so until 1946, albeit there was a temporary unity in 1916.

Both county forces have always maintained a close professional relationship but the events of August 1859 were to prove that liaison between the forces was far superior to many.

In the summer of 1859 Jane Whitcroft married one Joseph Castle of Ware, Hertfordshire. The marriage was anything but peaceful and violent quarrels often erupted between the couple, resulting in Jane finally leaving her husband and returning home to her mother in York Street, Luton.

On Tuesday, 9th August 1859, Castle visited the town and spoke with his wife and mother-in-law and encouraged Jane to return to her marital home. It was in her best interests to do so, he told her, as he could provide for her in a better manner than she had been used to. The foolish Jane fell for Castle's tale and decided to return with her husband and make another go of the relationship.

The body of Jane Castle was found on the road leading from Luton to Summeries Hill, her throat cut from ear to ear. She had been the victim of a dreadful attack, with several stab wounds to the lower part of her neck. A blood-stained knife was found close to the scene and was handed to Superintendent Pope of the Bedfordshire Force who was in overall charge of the investigation. It was clear from the outset that the knife was the murder weapon and it was quickly identified as the property of Joseph Castle, the victim's husband. Pope contacted his Hertfordshire colleagues and requested their assistance in apprehending the suspect. A full description of Joseph Castle was given and the Hertfordshire force agreed to assist in any way they could. Officers visited his home address but found no-one there, and various hostelries in the area were also visited but all with negative results. The news that the police were looking for him soon reached Castle's hearing and he decided to give himself up. He refused to discuss the matter with them and simply stated that he had had a serious argument with his wife.

Castle was conveyed to Bedford where he was tried for murder. The jury took just 13 minutes to decide that he was guilty of murder; he was sentenced to death and executed on Saturday, 31st March 1860. Before his death he told a fellow prisoner that he had killed his wife because she had abused him and caused him to be most unhappy!

A curious event which illustrated some of the difficulties facing policemen took place on the outskirts of Tring in Hertfordshire in 1863 when a large group of rogues converged on the district from London. Among their ranks were the rough and ready bare-knuckle boxers banned from such activities in the capital. They and their followers believed the tranquillity of Hertfordshire provided an ideal location for their gambling activities, though all too often these fights resulted in one or more of the fighters receiving fatal injuries. News of the group's arrival reached the Tring police who at once responded, the duty officer sending a number of officers down to the scene and ordering the crowd to leave. The crowd and fighters dispersed quite peacefully and caught a train to Watford where they alighted and reassembled in the fields next to Loates Lane.

The gambling and fighting soon resumed as the gathering

cheered on their personal preference. Once again the police were informed and the duty superintendent delegated two constables to move the rabble on; it did not matter where so long as it was outside their own jurisdiction. The two constables soon arrived at the scene, but unfortunately for them the fighting was now a real blood and thunder affair which evoked great emotions amongst the assembled throng, who yelled out their disapproval at the officers' obvious intention to stop everything. They simply ignored the instructions of the two constables, who themselves were warned to clear off or face the consequences. The crowd far outnumbered the number of police on duty at that time, hence no further action was taken. Eventually the crowds dispersed, with varying degrees of damage caused to personal property as they revelled in drink and the euphoria of a good wager. The Chief Constable, Colonel Robertson demanded a full report of the incident and as a result of this he administered disciplinary action against the two constables and the duty superintendent. The latter was reduced to the rank of inspector, one of the constables was dismissed from the force and the other, an officer junior in service, took a reduction in pay of four shillings a week.

There was great public outrage at the severity of the punishment. Colleagues voiced their discontent and for the first time there was a real fear that the police might take matters into their own hands. In order to prevent this, Robertson's advisors told him that he must reinstate each officer as soon as possible. He strongly disagreed but eventually conceded that this was the only solution available to him, thus each man had his punishment quashed, all resumed work on full pay and at the substantive ranks held previously. Robertson was a robust disciplinarian who thought or cared little about the welfare of his subordinate ranks; he was Chief and whatever anyone else said, or thought about him mattered little. He was, for all his faults, a fairly efficient officer who liked things done his own way.

In 1880 he was replaced by Lieutenant Colonel H J Daniell who was similarly a strict disciplinarian, and he introduced a set of rules for his officers to adhere to. It was a similar situation in Bedfordshire where Captain Boultbee was replaced by Major Ashton Warner. Together the two forces created some curious but understandable rules which were intended to set high professional standards of policing. 'Any constable who is found guilty of neglect of duty shall be liable to a penalty of £10 and imprisonment with hard labour for one month.' Presumably this would be served alongside the very felons some officers had apprehended! 'Any officer leaving the force would have five shillings deducted from his wages in order to compensate for the cost of tailoring his uniform to fit his successor.' 'All officers at all times must practise complete sobriety, one instance of drunkenness would render the officer liable to dismissal from the force.' 'Married officers attending Divine Service are to wear plain clothes, single officers must wear full uniform; every man, unless on duty on a Sunday, must attend Divine Service.' 'Officers intending to marry must sign a written declaration that they are free from all debt and have furniture to the value of £20.'

Entering the 20th century, both forces have had their fair share of misfortune when it comes to acts of murder, most are horrific, all senseless, though perhaps the most contentious case is that which occurred in the Bedfordshire countryside in August 1961, now popularly known as the 'A6 Murder', and which is discussed fully in a later chapter.

Hertfordshire has its own catalogue of murders and infamous manhunts, not least that which occurred in 1966 after three horrific and senseless murders in the Shepherds Bush area of London. It was Friday, 12th August and Police Constable Geoff Fox, Detective Constable David Wombwell and Detective Sergeant Chris Head, all in plain clothes in an unmarked police car, had stopped an old blue-coloured Standard Vanguard estate car; it was 3.15 pm and the vehicle was in Braybrook Street. Head and Wombwell left the police car and approached the Vanguard which had three people on board. The occupants were all well known criminals, Harry Roberts, John Witney and John Duddy. As the officers made their enquiries Roberts produced a gun and shot Wombwell in the left eye, killing him instantly. Chris Head attempted to run back to the police car but Roberts fired a shot into the fleeing Chris Head's back. The sergeant fell to the ground in front of the police car. Duddy meanwhile, ran directly up to the driver's window of the vehicle and let three rounds off, one of which killed Geoff Fox. The unfortunate officer had been sitting with his foot on the clutch and the car in gear, thus when he was killed he released pressure from the clutch allowing the pedal to rise and propel the vehicle forward, its front wheels running over the prostrate body of Chris Head. The vicious killers fled the scene, but as they did witnesses took down the registration number of their vehicle, PGT 726.

The resultant check confirmed the registered owner as Witney who was immediately arrested. Witney confessed the identities of his accomplices; Duddy was arrested in Glasgow but Roberts had gone to ground. On 16th August police circulated some 16,000 posters bearing Roberts' picture upon them, added to which was a reward of £1,000 for his capture. These posters resulted in over 6,000 reported sightings. In mid November of the same year police were notified of an empty hide located in some undergrowth in Thorley Wood, Bishops Stortford. A full forensic examination was carried out revealing a solitary fingerprint which was quickly identified as that of Harry Roberts. The following morning some 130 police officers systematically searched the area and within one hour Roberts had been arrested after being found hiding in a disused hangar close

Harry Roberts' lair in Thorley Wood, Bishops Stortford in 1966. The murder of three policemen shocked the nation and led to an intensive manhunt. Roberts was arrested nearby.

to Nathan's Wood. He was arrested by Sergeants Smith and Thorne.

The murder of the three policemen was instrumental in the foundation of the Police Dependant Trust, formed to assist families of police officers killed on duty, which in recent years has been sadly overused.

Today both Hertfordshire and Bedfordshire are policed by highly efficient officers who are totally professional in everything they do. Like every police force they have their share of problems when it comes down to the nitty gritty of fighting crime but overall both forces are successful in this field, serving their respective communities most admirably. The media would have us believe that murder and acts of violence are much more prevalent in today's society, but, as these stories show, life in the past could be just as dangerous.

THE HODDESDON RIPPER

IN 1807 the town of Hoddesdon, in the east of Hertfordshire, was shocked by the horrific news of a double
murder in its very midst. Our story, however, begins in
1788 with the birth of one Thomas Simmons, whose father
was a shoemaker by trade. The family were of a respectable
nature and were well respected within this tight community.

Mr Simmons senior was eventually forced to take up the
plough as a source of income. The shoe trade was all very
well but it was a costly occupation which tended to have a
slow turnover of trade and, unfortunately, his shoes were
too well made. Once a pair was purchased they lasted, so it
was a good while before customers returned for a further
pair. This financial disaster all but destroyed the family
unity, but being a God-fearing and hard-working man
Simmons would not let such setbacks defeat him. Hence he
worked the land for the local gentry. Sadly, however, the
change of occupation affected his health and he duly died at
some time around the turn of the century.

The young Thomas Simmons was put to work at an early
age for a Mr Boreham at his family home. He resided there
for several years and one could foresee a good secure future
for him within the household, but Thomas was not blessed
with much commonsense. He regularly abused fellow workers and servants at the house and on more than one occasion
was suspected of stealing from the household. In conse-

quence Mr Boreham had little alternative but to release him
from his service and into an unforgiving world. Simmons,
now aged 19, managed to obtain further employment at
Messrs Christie and Co, brewers, and there he worked for
several months.

Thomas Simmons was a normal young man as far as the
natural ways of the world were concerned, and although he
possessed a permanent pathetic grin upon his face he was
able to converse fairly well with members of the opposite
sex. For some time whilst at the Boreham household he had
been having a sexual relationship with Elizabeth Harris, a
maidservant. She was a great deal older than he but had
enjoyed the comforts provided by a younger man, including
the attention he paid her. Once he had been released from
employment at the house, however, Elizabeth wanted little
more to do with him; her employment meant much more to
her than sexual encounters which were never going to lead
anywhere. Most certainly she realised that Simmons was
never going to be the sort of person who could support her
and provide for her in the manner she had always dreamed
of. Thomas Simmons saw the relationship from a slightly
different perspective; he was deeply involved and enjoyed her
company and it was his intention that one day they should
be married. At no stage did he realise that the older woman
was using him.

Simmons blamed Mr Boreham for the break up of his
affair, and on several occasions when in drink he returned to
the house and threatened the family with harm unless he was
permitted to speak with Elizabeth Harris. On each occasion
he was escorted from the premises by members of the household staff upon the instruction of Mr Boreham. It never
struck him that Elizabeth concurred with her employer's
decision.

On Tuesday, 20th October 1807, the Boreham household
organised an evening party at their home. The company

included his four daughters, Anne, Elizabeth, Sarah and Mrs Warner, who was married to a brass-founder, and also Mrs Hummerstone, the caretaker landlady of The Black Lion public house in the town. They had gathered in the parlour where they sat and talked about local and national matters of importance. The evening was going very well and the party atmosphere was relaxed. They could not know how this relaxation was to be shattered.

It was around a quarter past nine in the evening when the group heard a commotion at the rear of the house. It was the ranting and raving of Thomas Simmons, who stood in the stone yard. Elizabeth Harris looked out of a window and saw him. She felt it safer to retire into the scullery, but unfortunately she had been spotted by her ex-lover who at once rushed to the rear door behind which she stood. He attempted to open the door but she refused to let him in.

Simmons became irate and uncontrollable. He shouted out obscenities and threats towards those inside the house, then suddenly, without further warning, he thrust his right hand, armed with a long bladed knife, through a small lattice window towards Elizabeth Harris, who screamed out in horror. The knife missed her arm but caused her to freeze with fear. The scream alerted those elsewhere in the house. Mrs Hummerstone, who as the landlady of a public house was used to dealing with ruffians, be they male or female, was first to the rear door. She stood rooted to the spot as Thomas Simmons forced his way past Elizabeth Harris and into the house brandishing a knife in his right hand. Before poor Mrs Hummerstone could do or say anything, Simmons thrust the knife deep into her throat, causing blood to spurt all over the walls and floor. Not satisfied with this he ripped open the left side of her throat. Mrs Hummerstone fell to the floor, her clothes scarlet as the blood pumped from the gaping gash.

Simmons left the body where it was, running into the

parlour where most of the party still remained. He threatened to rip them all open, waving his bloodstained knife in the air. Without further warning he seized hold of Mrs Warner and stabbed her continually in the throat, ripping it open; once again blood spurted out of the wound, saturating Simmons and the surrounding floor and walls. He continued to tear at Mrs Warner and stabbed her in the breast several times, ensuring that the ghastly deed was complete.

During these horrors the younger female members of the family had rushed to an upstairs room in the house and secured themselves to the best of their ability. Unfortunately, the aged Mrs Boreham could not escape so swiftly. Simmons leapt at her, plunging his knife deep into her neck. He then saw Mr Boreham making his escape into the kitchen. Pulling the knife from Mrs Boreham's neck he gave chase after the old man, during which he became entangled with a female servant who lunged at him. She received several wounds to her hand and arm in the attack, but managed to escape into the street and screamed 'Murder!' until almost the whole of the town was awoken by her terrified cries.

Thomas Simmons fled from the house but rather foolishly remained in the immediate vicinity, taking sanctuary in a barn in the grounds of Boreham's house. After a few minutes the townspeople began to arrive at the house and discovered the savage butchery carried out by the young man. The immediate fear of the local residents was the precise whereabouts of the killer. News of the atrocities committed by Simmons spread through the town, creating panic.

The local doctor turned out and duly pronounced Mrs Warner and Mrs Hummerstone dead; old Mrs Boreham, although in a deep state of shock and having a deep laceration to her throat, was not fatally wounded, although the memory of the attack was to live with her for the rest of her days. The young maidservant had the injuries to her hand and arm treated and after a number of hours things were beginning to get back to some form of normality in the Boreham household.

A search for Thomas Simmons was organised; he had last been seen running into the rear stone yard of the premises, hence the search commenced there. Each outhouse was nervously checked by a number of men who must have been equally as frightened as Thomas Simmons, they had seen what he was capable of and were not about to put themselves forward as his next victim. Eventually after a very short period one of the teams reported that someone was hiding in a cow-crib in the barn. Large groups of men hurried there and tentatively peered into the darkness in an attempt to locate their quarry. It was decided that the best option would be to attempt to coerce him out through talking to him.

Simmons lay terrified. He had calmed down after his ten minutes of insanity and realised the seriousness of his situation, yet what alternatives did he have, he was all but dead, should he fight for it or quietly give himself up? His thoughts were suddenly jolted by the shouts of the throng who told him to give himself up before any more harm was done. The next thing anyone knew was that Thomas Simmons was climbing out of the cow-crib and calmly walking towards the men. He told them that he was not armed and that he would do as he was told. He was extremely confused and one has to suspect, insane.

The groups of men who had a few minutes previously been like frightened mice were now all as brave as lions. The danger had disappeared, they knew where the killer was and that he posed no threat to them. Like heroes returning from battle this group of men marched their prisoner back into the town and to The Bell public house, where Thomas Simmons was handcuffed and bound and kept under guard until the following morning.

During the hours of darkness a number of persons visited the pub in order to view the prisoner and one can only

Thomas Simmons in gaol as he awaited trial in 1808. The long overcoat he wears does not quite conceal the leg irons.

suspect that Simmons was to suffer several beatings during his period of detention there. The following morning Mr Fairfax of The Black Bull public house visited the prisoner. Fairfax was a respected citizen of Hoddesdon and acted on behalf of the authorities in as much as he ensured that the prisoner was handed over to the constable of the parish. Fairfax entered the tiny room where Simmons lay uncomfortably on the floor and was horrified to see that the prisoner had a purple coloured face and had all but expired. Acting swiftly Fairfax cut loose the ligatures which bound him and allowed his circulation to resume. Simmons was then bound in a more humane manner, thus preserving his life until his trial and hopefully the suitable horrors which faced him once found guilty.

Simmons was taken before a local magistrate and committed for trial on the charge of murder; he was then conveyed to Hertford gaol until the day of his trial which had been set for Friday, 4th March 1808. The day quickly arrived and Simmons was brought before Mr Justice Heath. Amazingly, the Boreham family refused to press charges against Simmons for the murder of their daughter, Mrs Warner. The family were Quakers and quite simply believed that they should turn the other cheek rather than seek retribution via official justice, thus Simmons was tried only for the murder of Mrs Hummerstone.

Simmons had no defence for his actions and simply claimed as he had all along, that it was not his doing, he had been forced into it by Mr Boreham and Elizabeth Harris, both of whom had mistreated and verbally abused him. The story had little effect upon the jury who knew they were looking at a double murderer. The various authorities gave their evidence, describing the wounds caused to Mrs Hummerstone. The jury took but a few minutes to find Thomas Simmons guilty of murder and Mr Justice Heath sentenced him to death. On Monday, 7th March 1808 the

Hoddesdon Ripper, Thomas Simmons had his life taken away in a more humane manner than he deserved. Right to the end he maintained an air of calmness, accepting his fate.

THE
WICKED CRIME
OF LUCY LOWE

IN the mid Victorian period Stagsden, a few miles west of Bedford, was an industrious place, not only from an employment point of view, but also in its delight in gossip. There were those who felt that nothing escaped their attention, yet none of them anticipated murder within their village.

At approximately 20 minutes to six on the evening of Monday, 20th March 1876 a gamekeeper was out shooting in the Stagsden Side Gate plantation when he discovered a black parcel hidden in the undergrowth. Inquisitively he prodded at the wrapping, which was of a cloth-type material and subsequently proved to be a woman's black skirt. Opening the parcel the gamekeeper recoiled in horror as he saw before him the body of a young child.

Hurrying back to the village, the gamekeeper raised the alarm and the police were notified and duly attended, as did Doctor Swinson from Turvey. The body was examined but there were no obvious signs of maltreatment. Doctor Swinson decided that death had been caused by asphyxiation, and this was later confirmed at the post-mortem.

Police Sergeant Mardlin made enquiries in the local area but no-one within the village had seen or heard of anyone suffering difficulties that would cause them to murder their

Stagsden Side Gate Plantation today. It was here in 1876 that a gamekeeper discovered the body of a child, wrapped in a woman's skirt.

own flesh and blood. Numerous villages were visited but none provided any information which might have assisted Mardlin in his investigations.

Eventually he got the breakthrough he required. He heard of a young woman by the name of Lucy Lowe who had recently given birth to a child in Bedford and had mysteriously farmed out the child to relatives in Derby. The Lowes were a Stagsden family and her parents were horrified by such reports and refused to accept the possibility that their daughter could commit murder. Apart from that, she was working in London.

Mardlin commenced background enquiries into the life of Lucy Lowe. He found that she had been married twice; her first husband had died shortly after their marriage, her second husband more or less deserted her and the three children which had been born of the relationship. These children were now in the Bedford Workhouse. At some time in 1875 she had managed to gain employment at a large residence in Hampstead, London, for a family by the name of Kirkham. She was accepted as being a quiet and good employee who caused little trouble for her employers; she had the occasional boyfriend but no-one who would cause concern.

On 3rd January 1876 Lucy had left the Kirkhams, advising them that she had obtained a position working for her uncle in Bedford. She thanked the family for their support and promised to maintain contact. The Kirkhams were upset at losing such a good employee but resigned themselves to the thought that as long as Lucy was happy then they could not object. In fact, Lucy Lowe was an inveterate liar. She had no job in Bedford, her actual reason for leaving the Kirkhams was that she was pregnant.

Lucy found accommodation in Bedford at number 66 Greyfriars Walk, where she lodged with Mrs Priscilla Hull. On 26th February she gave birth to a baby girl. Within a few days of the birth Lucy was again telling untruths. She informed Mrs Hull that the child was going to be raised by her relatives in Derby. As a result of this, on 11th March 1876 Mrs Hull took Lucy and her child to Bedford railway station and put her on a train bound for Turvey. Later that day, at 1.30 pm Lucy Lowe arrived in Stagsden, at her parents' house, without her child. Lucy told her parents that she had just returned from London and thought she would call in. Her parents knew nothing of her residing in Bedford, nor that she had left the Kirkhams' employment. Perhaps more importantly, they had not the slightest idea that she had been pregnant.

Lucy stayed at Stagsden until the horrific discovery of the baby's body was made on 20th March. Realising that it would be foolish to leave the area too soon, she remained a further two days. On 22nd March she visited Mrs Hull and told her that the child had been handed over to the relatives in Derby and that she was going back to London. The following day she did, and managed to secure her previous employment with the Kirkhams.

Sergeant Mardlin, armed with this information, obtained the Kirkhams' Hampstead address and on 4th March he travelled to London and the Kirkhams' abode. There he spoke with the Reverend Joshua Kirkham and explained to him his reason for travelling to London; it was his intention to arrest Lucy Lowe on the charge of murder. Kirkham refused to believe the policeman's story. To the best of his knowledge Lucy had not given birth to a child in the past few months. Mardlin told him that the girl had told lies not only to him but to her family and friends. Kirkham denied Mardlin access and called the Metropolitan Police to the house, believing that they would support him rather than the Bedford sergeant. He was mistaken.

The authorities were allowed into the house and Lucy Lowe was brought to see them. Mardlin took hold of her arm and informed her that she was under arrest on suspicion of the murder of her three week old child. Kirkham asked to see the arrest warrant, under the misapprehension that one was required. When Mardlin told him that he did not require one, the Reverend then refused to let Mardlin take Lucy away. He pulled on her arm until officers from the Metropolitan Police intervened and explained that Mardlin was acting under correct authority and that no warrant was required. Kirkham himself was threatened with arrest if he should continue to obstruct Mardlin and after receiving a verbal warning from those officers present, he relented, realising that he was being foolish to doubt the police.

Lucy Lowe was tried at the Bedford summer assizes on 3rd July 1876. The background to the crime was revealed and

Lucy Lowe escaped the death penalty for the murder of her baby.

duly discussed at great length. Evidence was given that clothing found on the child's remains had been removed from Mrs Kirkham's wardrobe by Lucy Lowe, and a singular piece of ticking found upon the baby's body matched with

some found amongst Lowe's personal possessions at the time
of her arrest. Mrs Hull was called to testify against Lowe.
She spoke of the numerous lies the woman had told and of
how when she left Greyfriars Walk she had failed to take any
of the baby's clothing or its feeding bottle, as though she
knew that the child would no longer require these.

The defence counsel quite simply stated that the charges
were a gross misinterpretation of the facts. The unfortunate
victim of this incident was Lucy Lowe herself, it was
claimed, the child having died of natural causes. In her panic
she left it in the undergrowth, the action of a disturbed and
concerned mother! Lucy Lowe did not take the witness
stand, however she made a specially prepared statement
which was read out to the court: 'On the 14th day of March
when I left Turvey station the weather was very cold. I
wrapped the child in three shawls and carried it along until
I got through Stagsden Side Gate when the child had a fit and
died almost immediately. I was very frightened and I left it
where it was afterwards found.'

The jury retired and within twelve minutes returned a
verdict of guilty against Lowe. She was sentenced to death.

This story does not end here, for the jury took mercy upon
the child-killer and submitted a recommendation to the authorities that the death penalty should be commuted and that
a term of imprisonment would be more appropriate. The
appeal was granted and Lucy Lowe escaped the grip of the
executioner's noose.

Did Lucy Lowe tell the truth about how her child died? If
she did then a huge amount of evidence against her must
have been wrong. Doctor Swinson confirmed that death had
been by suffocation, but could this have been caused by the
mother clutching the child so close to her breast that it
suffocated? I think not. Lucy Lowe deliberately murdered
her baby daughter. The 37 year old mother was indeed a
fortunate woman to escape her true punishment.

WITCH HUNT

THE most notorious era of witchcraft this country has ever known was without doubt during the 17th century, when witch-hunting reached almost epidemic proportions and anyone who did not conform to the basic ways of society was classed as a witch. Witchfinder General Matthew Hopkins, a lawyer from the Suffolk town of Ipswich, is perhaps the most famous of the witch prosecutors. Yet the hysteria which often accompanied witch hunts was to be seen again in Hertfordshire a century later. To visit the peaceful town of Tring today one can hardly imagine the atrocities which occurred there in 1751 as a result of a witchcraft scare.

On 18th April 1751 the peace and tranquillity of Hemel Hempstead, several miles away, was shattered by the news that two 'witches' from Tring who were regular visitors to Hemel had been found 'guilty' at an unofficial trial held by the townsfolk. The two witches were to be publicly ducked for their troubles. A notice to this effect was handed to the Hemel Hempstead town crier, William Dell, who dutifully expounded the news, and similar notices were read out at Winslow and Leighton Buzzard on market days.

The overseer of the parish of Tring heard the news of the punishment to be handed out and the accusations being brandished, and in an attempt to bring some sanity to the proceedings he announced that he would carry out his own investigations into the claims being made. The identity of the two suspects who had to suffer this awful torture had itself been subject to much speculation, however it took Barton very little time to ascertain that it was John and Ruth Osborne, a husband and wife. Both were known to Barton and, what must have been of more concern to him, their only apparent crime was that they rarely mixed with other members of the local community and maintained their own counsel. Barton realised that if the ducking were to proceed then serious harm would come to the unfortunate couple, so he made secret arrangements to have them moved out of their home and to a place of safety, on this occasion Tring workhouse.

On the prearranged date of the planned ducking, a crowd of somewhere in the region of 5,000 swarmed into the streets of Tring. News spread that the point of destination was the home of the Osbornes, but a search of those premises soon showed that they were absent, perhaps in hiding elsewhere. It is difficult to keep anything quiet within any kind of community and it was not too long before word spread that the Osbornes had been removed to the workhouse. The volatile crowd made their way to the old building and stood chanting and jeering in the street outside the main entrance door, screaming for the blood of the terrified Osbornes. Suddenly a loud crash was heard and a wall of the workhouse collapsed with the pressure of the swaying human force upon it. A number of persons were injured in this incident, which did not detract from the hatred felt towards the unfortunate couple within.

The leading agitator of this group, a man by the name of Colley, screamed out to the workhouse authorities that unless the Osbornes were released into their custody the workhouse would fall. This signalled a barrage of stones hurled towards the premises, smashing windows. The workhouse master, realising the imminent danger, told Colley that the people for whom they searched had left the premises. The agitator refused to accept this and demanded that he and a number of others be allowed to search the workhouse, and before a reply could be given several of the throng ran into the premises and searched every room and closet but could find no trace of the Osbornes. A hole in the plaster ceiling of one of the cupboard spaces was found and Colley insisted that it be searched, so one of the group launched himself through the hole in the ceiling and was enveloped in the darkness beyond, but within a few minutes he emerged – without the Osbornes.

The situation was rapidly getting out of control, and the threat to pull the workhouse down suddenly seemed quite feasible. With this in mind, the workhouse master felt he had no alternative but to admit where the Osbornes were; he had sent them to the vestry room of the nearby church. Colley and his army proceeded there and duly located their quarry.

The crowd dragged John and Ruth Osborne to a pond known as Marlston Mere, where the couple were stripped semi-naked and tied and gagged separately. Ruth Osborne was tied with a rope secured tightly beneath her armpits; she was then thrown to the ground and left at the mercy of Colley who took great enjoyment in abusing her (verbally and physically). Colley requested two volunteers to step forward. Two men did so and were duly instructed to drag Ruth Osborne into the dark and muddy pond water by her securing ropes. Ruth was pulled through the pond several times and on each occasion she was submerged; unable to maintain any buoyancy without the use of her limbs, she was now at the mercy of the maniac Colley. Colley ordered the two men to leave her in the deepest part of the pond and approached her, prodding at her torso with a large stick, as he turned her over and over in the water like a pig on a spit. Just when Ruth Osborne must have been begging that her Maker allow her to die, Colley ordered the two men to pull her out and lay her on the pond banking.

The unfortunate John Osborne had witnessed this act of

cruelty and knew that he would have to face a similar barbaric torture. He was dragged and submerged in the pond
water before being laid next to his exhausted wife. Ruth
Osborne was then forced to go through the agony one more
time, as too did her husband. Finally, Ruth, who was by this
time wrapped in a sheet in order to make it more difficult for
her to float, was dragged through for a third time. She
floundered in the middle of the pond and the sheet fell open,
exposing her body, which by this stage was devoid of all
personal clothing. Thomas Colley calmly waded up to her.
The realisation that the end was nigh seemed to stimulate
him and, like the Grim Reaper, he took his stick and
prodded Ruth on the breast, forcing her body beneath the
surface of the dirty water. There he held her for a few
minutes. Death must have come as some relief to Ruth
Osborne.

Thomas Colley showed no remorse for his callous actions.
He walked around the pond and collected monies from those
present as a reward for treating them to some sport!
Although various amounts of cash changed hands the
general mood of the crowd had altered. Many were sickened
by what they had witnessed, some even turned against
Colley, hurling insults at him for his lack of respect towards
another human being. Ruth Colley was dragged from the
pond and laid next to the body of her husband, who had
lapsed into a state of unconsciousness.

Mr Foster, the local surgeon was called and examined the
body of the dead woman. No wound could be found either
internal or external, though an amount of skin was rubbed
off one breast, and he announced death by virtue of
suffocation from water and mud!

The authorities were informed of the incident. John
Osborne survived the attack but the mental torture he
suffered was to ensure that his life was all but over. Thomas
Colley was apprehended and questioned; he denied the

offence and intimated that if he were guilty then so were the assembled crowd who had all supported his actions. He was taken to Hertford prison, tried and duly found guilty of murder, then sentenced to death. The day prior to his execution, Colley was removed from Hertford prison and taken to the St Albans lock-up. During this location exchange he was escorted by 100 men of the Oxford Blues who were under

Witch hunts continued in country districts well into the 19th century, often leading to the mistreatment and sometimes the death of innocent old women, as this engraving from The Illustrated Police News in the 1870s shows.

the command of seven officers.

At five o'clock on the morning of 24th August 1751, Colley was taken from the confines of his cell and placed in a chaise along with the hangman; he was then transported to the Tring gallows. As he arrived there his wife and daughter were permitted a final few moments with him. Normally this would have taken place in the privacy of the condemned cell, but Colley was not afforded such an opportunity. The visit of his family appeared to give him great cause for concern. The minister of Tring assisted him in his last moments, but still Colley displayed no remorse for what he had done, it seems that in his own mind he believed that he had rid the world of a messenger of evil which took the form of a woman. Suddenly, that fateful bang of the gallows trap door echoed through the streets of Tring. Thomas Colley was no more, his neck snapping almost immediately.

After a short time Colley's body was cut down and hung in chains at a place called Gubblecut, on the outskirts of Tring, as a reminder to those who took justice into their own hands that their punishment could be equally horrific.

WHO KILLED
MARY ANN FAVEL?

IN the 1870s Lamsey was a small district of Leighton Buzzard, consisting of a few streets of mainly terraced houses. Thomas Whitley, the town lamplighter who worked for the Leighton Buzzard Gas Company, was wearily tramping the streets of Lamsey in the early morning hours of Sunday, 15th October 1876. It was a cool fresh morning and there was a light drizzly rain. Whitley must have had his thoughts upon his family and a good hearty breakfast later that morning – certainly his task did not require him to maintain committed concentration. Often as he passed through the streets he would hear the personal activities which occasionally occurred in local residents' houses. Domestic harmony or disputes, he had heard and seen the lot; it was perhaps all that he could find to interest him on his travels.

It was about 3.30 am as Whitley walked through the streets when he heard the sound of what he initially thought was someone screaming, 'Murder!' He stopped in his tracks. There was a loud scream but he could not decide where it was emanating from, the streets and alleyways tending to create echoes. He wondered about the scream, it seemed slightly more panicky than those during the regular disputes he overheard, but there was no further sound and Whitley continued on his way, believing that he had heard just another family quarrel.

Thomas Whitley was not the only one to have cause for alarm that morning. Betty Scrivener was enjoying a peaceful deep sleep when at sometime around 4 am she heard a loud thump coming from the house next door. It was loud enough to cause vibration to her bedroom furniture and it appeared to be caused by something of considerable weight being dropped onto the wooden floorboards of the house next door. The tired woman thought that perhaps she had imagined the noise and so snuggled back down between the sheets and resumed her slumbers.

At 5 am the same morning, Charlie Greeves had just finished a long night shift on the Great Western Railway, where he worked as a flagman. Greeves had worked for the company for a few years and had been on the night shift for quite a while; the shift suited him, allowing him time at home with his family and to carry out extra work throughout the day to supplement his income. Greeves was a Leighton Buzzard man through and through, he knew most people in the town, so when he saw a woman sitting on the doorstep of Johnny Johnson's house he wondered what was going on. The woman, who appeared to be middle aged, had a red shawl covering her head, but even from a distance it was obvious that she was extremely upset and was crying. Charlie Greeves approached the woman and asked if everything was all right; he knew that she was not a member of the Johnson household and wondered if she was perhaps lost or, even worse, had been subjected to some kind of attack. Bending down he took hold of the woman by the shoulders and looked her straight in the face. Despite his attention and obvious concern the woman would not speak with Greeves, and realising that she did not require his interference, he told her that he would leave her to her own thoughts and continued on his way home, somewhat puzzled by the woman's condition. He consoled himself with the thought that if she had wanted his assistance then she would have asked for it;

he had done everything he could to help.

Unbeknown to any of these three innocent parties, they were witnessing events on the periphery of murder. If only they had known at the time then the authorities could have reacted more promptly, albeit the crime was complete and there was little anyone could have done to save the victim.

It was shortly after 6.30 am, Jane Favel told the police, when she found the badly burnt body of her daughter, Mary Ann Favel. The 26 year old girl was found lying prostrate in a downstairs room; she was surrounded by her burnt clothing which had been reduced to ash, but although badly burned the body was still easily recognisable. Mary's beautiful hair had all but gone, reduced to stubble, and the body had a purplish brown appearance, her face bearing a grimace of pain. Clutched tightly in her right hand were a number of small coins to the value of tenpence halfpenny.

After the police were notified, Superintendent Shepherd and Sergeant Olden plus three constables arrived on the scene and the house was sealed off, no-one allowed to enter or leave the premises without police authority. Shepherd called out Doctor Harris who duly examined the remains and certified Mary Ann dead; the body was then removed to the local morgue.

The police investigation began to click into gear. Shepherd looked for signs of forced entry into the house but could find no such evidence. He then briefly interviewed each of the six other persons who had been sleeping in the house that fateful morning. Something was amiss, for not one person in the household would admit to hearing or smelling anything untoward during the time in question, yet the house clearly smelled of burnt flesh. There was also a slight aroma of benzoline, which it was ascertained had been poured over Mary Ann Favel in order to set her alight. It was almost impossible to believe that not one individual had smelled anything, yet this was the claim. Shepherd held strong suspicions about Jane Favel, the 51 year old mother of the dead girl. Her story altered during the chat he had with her and she did not give the appearance of a grieving mother. George Favel, Mary Ann's brother, had also altered his story to fit in with that of his mother, as too did Catherine Samuel, a friend of George's who had been staying at the house at the time. As there were no signs of a break-in, Shepherd suspected someone within, and he duly arrested the three named individuals on suspicion of murder.

The trio were brought before the Leighton bench prior to being committed to the Warwick Assizes where they stood trial on 4th December 1876. There was very little in the way of evidence against them and it was no surprise when the Grand Jury declared that there was no true bill to answer and they were each discharged.

Jane Favel returned to Leighton Buzzard a happy woman, though it was perhaps uppermost in her mind that public opinion might be against her on her return to the town. To see if this was the case she visited her old friend, a 70 year old by the name of Mrs Chandler. Jane Favel was made welcome and invited into the house. Mrs Chandler already had some company and the three ladies sat and drank some beer before Jane Favel asked that Mrs Chandler escort her round to her home as she was too frightened to return alone. She agreed and duly put on her coat and walked into the street with Jane Favel by her side. After a few steps Jane Favel turned the conversation to the sad loss of her daughter. Mrs Chandler replied something to the effect that someone must have committed the foul deed as there was no reason for Mary to take her own life in such a manner. Jane Favel suddenly blurted out, 'It was me. She would not give me the tenpence halfpenny, I needed it, she wanted to get her hat dyed, so I went out to the barn after her and hit her on the head with a stick. She fell. I then went back into the house for a while, afterwards I went back to the barn thinking she might be dead. I dragged her into the house again. Then I poured oil over her, I could not stop in the house after what I had done, so I went and sat on the doorstep.'

The case surrounding the mysterious death of the young girl had caused uproar in the streets of Leighton Buzzard. Everyone, it seemed, was horrified at the inhumane actions of the killer and most people readily accepted that Jane Favel was somehow implicated, yet no-one could prove it. Mrs Chandler advised the police of what she had been told by Favel, but it was at that time insufficient inasmuch as it was hearsay evidence. The local authorities offered a reward of some £100 for information which would identify or lead to the arrest of the evil killer or killers. The authorities knew that they were close to proving the case but needed that little bit more just to swing it their way. The enticement of serious financial reward was more than sufficient to encourage someone to come forward. Another member of the Favel family, Isaac, who was in the house on the night in question was coerced into contacting the police and providing a statement which would give sufficient grounds for the police to re-arrest Jane Favel.

On Saturday, 7th April 1877 Jane Favel was once again charged with the murder of her daughter, the initial hearing taking place on Friday, 13th April 1877. One of the first witnesses called to give evidence was Doctor Harris, who explained to the packed courtroom just how Mary Ann Favel had suffered. Benzoline from an oil lamp had been poured over her body and set alight whilst she was still alive. He further commented that he found it curious that not one person within the house had smelled anything extraordinary, there were gaps beneath most of the inner doors in the premises which would allow the fumes to pervade the house and as for the stench itself, well, that was one of the most distinctive smells one could ever imagine. To supplement this observation the prosecutor, Mr Mitchell, stated that he found it altogether unbelievable that with all those present in the house, not one had noticed anything suspicious.

The prosecution then discussed where the benzoline might have come from; it was generally used in oil lamps, a number of which were found within the house. Jane Favel had told Doctor Harris that she had not used her own lamp for over twelve months, similarly she told Sergeant Olden and later, Superintendent Shepherd an identical tale. Other evidence indicated that Jane Favel was in fact mistaken; Matilda Favel, her daughter-in-law, told the court that she had been sent by Jane Favel to purchase a quantity of benzoline for the lamps. William Barnton told how he made his living selling the liquid, he explained how highly inflammable it was and that it would take but five or six minutes to burn out within a combustible atmosphere, when the spirit would simply evaporate.

Jane Favel was committed for trial at the Bedfordshire Assizes. All the evidence seemed to be strongly against her. Mrs Chandler was called to inform the court how she had more or less confessed the murder, and a further witness corroborated this testimony. Whilst Chandler was giving evidence in the witness box, Jane Favel screamed out at her, 'You liar, it is all lies, do not believe her.' The weakness of this confession as evidence was immediately identified and seized upon by the defence counsel. Chandler had repeated it to her friend Mrs White, who in turn had repeated it verbatim to Sergeant Olden. The counsel asked both women to repeat their testimonies and both altered their stories, not by a great deal, but sufficient to cast doubts upon their accuracy. Mrs Chandler was in her seventies and her memory was not as sharp as it had been. She gave her evidence in an excellent manner but on cross examination laboured greatly through her hearing problems. It was this defect which destroyed her evidence, the defence simply claimed that she had misheard what Jane Favel had been saying.

The prosecution introduced Thomas Whitley, who had heard the shout of 'Murder' whilst passing through the area, but again the defence were able to cast doubts upon the witness's credibility. Why had he not carried out any further investigations into the scream, surely as a law-abiding citizen it was his responsibility to do so? He could provide no reasonable answer to this suggestion. Mrs Scrivener, who had been awakened by a loud thud in the house next door to her own property and where Mary Ann Favel resided, was further discredited, the defence asking where the thud had emanated from. 'An upstairs room,' came the reply. Mary Ann Favel's body was found downstairs, hence it appeared that Mrs Scrivener's account was of little consequence. She denied hearing any cry of 'Murder', which did little to enhance the case for the prosecution.

The jury retired to consider their verdict. It seemed quite clear that Jane Favel had murdered her daughter, yet had the prosecution been able to prove as much during the trial? After an absence of over one hour, the jury returned with a 'Not Guilty' verdict. The mother screamed her delight as she walked from the courtroom, a free woman.

A few years later Jane Favel confessed her guilt to another source, an off duty police officer. She described how she had hit her daughter over the head before setting fire to the body in order to destroy the evidence. Although it cannot be proved, it seems probable that both women were common prostitutes. Young Mary Ann was making much more money and taking business from her mother. Eventually Jane Favel had asked her for money and the quarrel erupted resulting in the murder of Mary Ann, which is intrinsically the same confession expounded to Mrs Chandler. Jane Favel was undoubtedly most fortunate to escape the gallows. Had it not been for the poor presentation of the case for the prosecution then she may well have met a more just reward.

MURDER IN
GILLS HILL LANE

WITHIN the parochial boundaries of the quiet village of Elstree in Hertfordshire lie the bodies of two separate victims of murder. The first victim buried in the old churchyard is one Martha Reay, shot dead by a jealous lover outside a theatre in London's Covent Garden. Her killer, Reverend James Hackman, was executed at Tyburn in 1779. The second victim of murder died some 46 years later, a man by the name of William Weare.

Weare's story starts, however, with one John Thurtell, born on 21st December 1794, the son of Alderman Thomas Thurtell of Norwich who had twice been mayor of the same city. After a brief career at sea and in the army, by 1814 John Thurtell was living and working in Norwich where he manufactured bombazine (a twilled or corded dress fabric), which was seemingly quite a profitable business. Thurtell, though, was something of an impulsive man who regularly squandered his profits on alcohol and gambling which in turn caused him to accumulate several large debts.

Later that same year he visited a wealthy London family to whom he sold fabric and goods to the value of £400; he boasted about the sale and it was not long before his creditors got to hear about it and demanded that he begin to repay some of his outstanding debts. The creditors in fact never received a single penny, as Thurtell concocted an imaginative tale explaining that he had been robbed by footpads on his return to Norwich – they had stolen all the money. The lies were blatant and those who suffered from Thurtell's financial squanderings were incensed enough to attempt to resolve matters themselves. If he could not pay by cash then his innards would suffice! The people to whom he owed money were of the unsavoury kind who might well fulfil their promises and Thurtell fled to London, taking his longstanding girlfriend Mary Dodson with him. There he met up with his brother and together they took over a tavern in Watling Street. On 26th January 1823 the premises burnt down, resulting in an insurance claim of £2,000 which was settled within a few weeks.

Armed with some ready cash the brothers then purchased another tavern, The Black Boy, in Long Acre, London. John Thurtell continued to be a compulsive and heavy gambler, he ran up further debts in his brother Henry's name and within a few months he had become involved in many underworld activities and nurtured his keen interest in boxing, not the professional sport as we now know it, but bare-knuckle fights which attracted the serious gambling fraternity. Thurtell's obvious intention was to make money from his fighters, who he personally trained.

It was through his involvement with the underworld that Thurtell met with another rogue by the name of Joseph Hunt, who coincidentally was also the manager of a public house (the Army and Navy Tavern). He had served several terms of penal servitude for his part in thefts and deceptions and knew the inside of Newgate prison very well. The two men were similar in many ways, unscrupulous, liars and above all, ruthless. Hunt fancied himself as something of a dandy. He enjoyed dressing in fine clothing, which enabled him to live out his dreams of wealth and power and, although he was married, enjoyed the company of women of loose morals.

William Weare was himself something of a gambling man

and he frequently mixed in the circles used by Thurtell and Hunt, who over a short period of time had become extremely friendly with each other. Weare was a solicitor and was slightly more educated than those with whom he mixed within the gambling dens of the metropolis. One evening when he met Thurtell at the gambling table, he actually took Thurtell for the sum of £300, which of course greatly angered the publican. Rumours began to circulate about an amount of money which Weare was thought to carry around with him; this personal bank was believed to be kept in a secret pocket beneath his waistcoat. It was the possibility that this fund existed which inspired Thurtell and Hunt to plan a vicious act of robbery.

On the evening of Thursday, 23rd October 1823 John Thurtell invited William Weare to a cottage in Gills Hill Lane, about three miles from Elstree. Weare was informed that he could enjoy some private shooting and a spot of gambling, and the offer was too good to refuse. Weare at once accepted and made the necessary arrangements in London. The cottage in fact belonged to another rogue by the name of Bill Probert, who was in on Thurtell and Hunt's plan to rob the unsuspecting Weare.

Early in the morning of Friday, 24th October 1823, two men answering the description of Thurtell and Hunt visited a pawnbroker's shop in Marylebone and purchased a pair of pocket pistols. Joseph Hunt then hired a horse and cart, advising the dealer that he required it for a brief visit to Dartford, Kent. He also asked the dealer if he knew where he could procure a sack and some good quality rope; he was given an address over the Westminster Bridge and duly acquired the said items.

John Thurtell, meanwhile, collected Weare from his lodgings. Weare had with him a green carpet bag containing a backgammon board and some personal items; he also took his double-barrel gun along in anticipation of the shooting.

The two men set off for Elstree in the horse and cart and along the way were overtaken by another horse and gig, upon which sat Probert and Hunt. The latter two, believing they were ahead of schedule, stopped off at a public house for some light refreshment, and possibly some Dutch courage which would enable them to carry out the robbery. Unwittingly the two men were in the inn longer than they anticipated, and Thurtell and Weare thundered by un-noticed.

After a short time Probert and Hunt emerged from the inn and continued on their way. Hunt was dropped off at Phillimore Lodge (between Radlett and Elstree on what is now the A5183) where he was expected to lie in wait for Thurtell and Weare. The obvious problem which they now faced and which neither rogue realised, was that Thurtell was actually ahead of Hunt.

After Probert dropped Hunt he continued along his way to his home in Gills Hill Lane, but as he approached it he met with John Thurtell. He naturally asked what Thurtell was doing there so soon. Thurtell told him that Weare was dead, he had killed him and Probert should go and fetch Hunt at once, which he did. Back in Gills Hill Lane, Thurtell rebuked Hunt for his foolishness, he also told him that the two pistols he purchased were little better than pop guns, he had fired one at Weare's cheek but it had glanced off without causing him any serious harm. He then described the terrible events of that night. Weare had jumped from the cart and run off down the lane pleading for mercy. Thurtell had chased him and a struggle had taken place during which Thurtell attempted to slit Weare's throat with his pocket penknife. This had failed but caused sufficient injury to render Weare stunned for a few minutes. Seizing the opportunity Thurtell had then driven the barrel of one of the pistols deep into Weare's brain and fired it.

It was now around 9 pm and the three men decided to go

to Probert's cottage where they could discuss the matter in relative security without attracting too much attention. Thurtell carried a green carpet bag with him. At Probert's cottage the trio ate heartily before again venturing out into the night. Mrs Probert was somewhat suspicious of her husband's antics at that time of night and demanded to know where he was going. Probert tamely informed her that they were off to visit a neighbour, Mr Nicholls. The men left and returned to the scene of Weare's murder. The solicitor's body was a sickening sight as it lay motionless and disfigured on the grass verge next to the gravel road. The body was dragged away from immediate view of the road and into a nearby field, where Weare's clothing was systematically searched and all items of value or identification were removed. With this done the men returned to Probert's cottage where Thurtell washed himself down; a stable boy asked him where the blood had come from but received no reply. For the rest of the evening the men sat with the Probert family and acted perfectly normally, indeed, Thurtell was the perfect gentleman – he gave Mrs Probert a gold chain, which had at one time had Weare's watch upon it.

Despite her pleasantness, Mrs Probert was not happy about Thurtell and Hunt. She bid the men goodnight as she feigned tiredness and retired to her upstairs bedroom. Stood by an upstairs window, she saw the three men leave the house and go to the stable where they took out a horse, and walk off up Gills Hill Lane. Within a few minutes the group returned, the horse carrying a heavy-looking sack upon its back. The men pulled the sack from the horse's back before dragging whatever the sack contained down towards the pond at the foot of the garden. The horse was returned to the stable and the group returned to the cottage. Once within, out of Mrs Probert's view, the evil trio then shared out Weare's property, managing to get £6 each, and the incriminating papers of identification were burnt in the fireplace.

An engraving showing John Thurtell dragging William Weare's body from the gig in Gills Hill Lane. (From The Trial of John Thurtell and Joseph Hunt, by Pierce Egan, London 1824)

At six the following morning, Thurtell and Hunt rose early and revisited the scene of the attack. They had somehow lost the murder weapons and obviously wished to get them back. As the two groped around in the undergrowth and hedgerow they were spotted by a group of workmen who asked what they were doing; Thurtell explained that their cart had almost overturned the previous evening and that they had lost some personal property in the grass as it slipped off the cart. With this explanation the pair then decided to leave the workmen to their own devices and returned to Probert's cottage. The workmen busied themselves by carrying out their own search for items of value, but what they did discover was not to their liking – a bloodstained penknife and a brain-splattered pistol, and an area of grass which appeared to be covered in blood.

Thurtell and Hunt meanwhile decided it would be best if they left the area at once and so collected the green carpet bag and returned to London, where Hunt took his newly acquired possessions back to his Golden Square lodgings. The two realised, however, that they would have to return to Hertfordshire to move the body to a more remote area, as the alarm was sure to be raised once the workmen found the pistol and penknife, so after laying low for one day they returned to Probert's cottage complete with spade.

Earlier on the same day of their return, Probert had cause to visit Mr Nicholls his neighbour. Nicholls informed him that something odd had taken place in Gills Hill Lane at around 8 pm the previous night, when a man named Smith claimed to have heard the sound of wheels and the report of a gun which was quickly followed by groaning noises. The worried Probert told Nicholls that he had neither seen nor heard anything that night and returned home somewhat rapidly. He was relieved to see Thurtell and Hunt and at once told them what had transpired with the neighbours.

Later that night the two men dragged Weare's body from

The interior of the Crown Court at Hertford as Thurtell and Hunt were brought up to plead. (Hertford Museum)

Probert's pond and cut all the clothing from it, leaving it totally naked. The corpse was then placed into a fresh sack and thrown onto the back of a gig. Much of the clothing was then cut into little pieces and distributed around the country-side. The sack was weighted down with heavy stones before being conveyed to Hill Slough (between Radlett and Elstree) and dumped into a deep muddy pond. Thurtell and Hunt knew that without a body there would be little chance of a conviction, hence they were somewhat relieved to finally get rid of it.

In the meantime, Mr Nicholls heard of the workmen's find in Gills Hill Lane, and a further tale of the visitor to Probert's cottage that evening being seen covered in blood. The inquisitive neighbour decided that he should inform the Hertfordshire magistrates of the facts as he knew them; this done it was decided that Bill Probert should be arrested as he obviously knew more than he was letting on. Upon being arrested Probert began to sing like a canary. He told the authorities everything that had transpired and that Thurtell and Hunt were the main conspirators in the crime, not him. From the information received from Probert, both John Thurtell and Joseph Hunt were arrested. Thurtell was questioned at length but denied all knowledge of the crime, claiming he was elsewhere when the murder took place. Hunt confessed everything, even taking the Bow Street Runners to the spot where the body had been dumped. A search of his lodgings revealed Weare's missing property.

Thurtell and Hunt were tried and found guilty of murder; Bill Probert turned King's Evidence and escaped justice for his part in the crime. Both men received the punishment of death.

John Thurtell was executed at Hertford before an estimated crowd of some 15,000, on Thursday, 9th January 1824, the hangman, 'Cheshire', having to pull on his feet more than a dozen times as his body swung from the gallows rope. Joseph Hunt appealed against his sentence and on 27th January 1824 had his sentence commuted to transportation for life to Australia, where he died in 1861. Bill Probert's escape from justice was shortlived as he was arrested for a horse-stealing offence on Friday, 18th February 1825, duly found guilty and executed on 20th June that same year.

Probert's cottage became a regular haunt for sightseers and souvenir hunters who flocked to it in their hundreds, removing various pieces over the years. So popular was it at one time that, some four years after the murder, Sir Walter Scott visited the scene whilst driving back to Scotland. The cottage itself lasted until some time around the 1880s when it had to be knocked down.

Gills Hill Lane has changed beyond all recognition, new houses now occupy most of the main sites of interest.

William Weare's grave still lies within Elstree churchyard and, like the other victim of murder whose remains lie close by, he died at the hands of an individual who harboured an obsession equally as destructive as jealousy, avarice.

MURDER MOST FOUL

IN 1819 the village barber in the Bedfordshire village of
Potton, Phillip Reynolds, became the proud father of a
fine baby girl, who was named Sarah. Reynolds was a
hard-working man who attempted to provide for his family,
but eventually the unfortunate barber succumbed to the
burden of debt. For many months he had procured necessi-
ties 'on tick' with the promise of payment at a later date, but
these promises were ill founded for Reynolds had no money.
He was forced to close the barber's shop and in 1825 he was
gaoled at Bedford for bad debts, a bitter blow to the
Reynolds family. Worse was to follow in 1826, when shortly
after his release from Bedford prison, the unfortunate Phillip
Reynolds died. The damp and miserable prison conditions
had seriously affected his health, which was none too good
before his gaol sentence. The stability of a father figure was
lost forever to young Sarah.

It would seem that sexual promiscuity was an accepted
part of the lifestyle of Sarah's mother. Certainly there were
a number of different male visitors to the family home whilst
husband Phillip was alive, and it is not beyond the realms of
possibility that Phillip Reynolds knew of his wife's affairs but
for reasons best known to himself preferred to ignore them.
Sarah, then, had a succession of men whom she would be
instructed to refer to as 'Uncle'; the poor child must have
found it difficult to understand why her mother continually

introduced new men into the house. Matters improved slightly when several months after her husband's death Mrs Reynolds remarried.

Despite the inadequacies of her mother, Sarah grew up to be a pretty and confident young woman. Her long silky auburn hair was generally worn in a bun, but from contemporary sketches it would seem that this did little to enhance her appearance and in fact seemed to age her. Being a tall girl Sarah possessed an elegant gait, and her dark brown eyes rounded off her beauty. Such a good-looking woman is seldom without an admirer and, following in her mother's footsteps, Sarah had numerous boyfriends.

In 1838 Sarah apparently settled down and married a local man, Simeon Mead. The couple remained in Potton for about two years before moving to nearby Tadlow in 1840. The reasons behind the move are uncertain but some claimed that Sarah had taken up an extra-marital relationship and that Simeon had found out and insisted upon moving to sever his wife's contact with her lover. Whatever the reason, it seems to have been of benefit to the couple's relationship as they were soon blessed with a child, a son. The euphoria of becoming parents was short-lived, however, as the child lived for just a few months.

This was a devastating time for Simeon, who worshipped the child. Both he and Sarah seemed greatly agitated by the loss, although it seems that Simeon mourned day and night, virtually turning into a recluse. Neighbours rallied round and attempted to ease the couple's pain with continued support and of course, much-needed sympathy, but no-one realised that beneath this obvious grief lay more serious domestic issues. Outwardly the couple had seemed content, but they had been at loggerheads for many months with Sarah generally agitating the domestic harmony. Like her mother, Sarah was sexually promiscuous; her flirtations with other men from the surrounding villages caused Simeon much grief.

Very suddenly, in October 1840, Simeon Mead passed away. The whole community were horrified and great sympathy was showered upon Sarah. Despite the curious death of her child, then husband, no-one seems to have suspected foul play, though the deaths had taken place within just a few weeks of each other. For a short time Sarah played the grieving widow whose life had been ruined.

Like her mother before her, Sarah took up another relationship within weeks of her husband's death. She was regularly seen in the company of a 23 year old labourer by the name of William Dazley. In February 1841, just four months after Simeon's death, the couple married and almost immediately escaped from the viperous tongues of Tadlow (which had begun to realise that all was not as it should be with the young woman) to a small house in Wrestlingworth, which is situated about three miles from Potton.

Sarah Dazley, as she was now known, was very much the dominant partner in the relationship. She insisted that Ann Mead, her dead husband's 14 year old sister should come to live with them, and William offered no objection to this and accepted the girl as part of his family responsibilities. As in her previous relationship the couple seemed quite happy; both were popular members of the community although some of the womenfolk held their suspicions as to Sarah's character, but provided she did not touch their husbands then there was no problem! Others were sceptical of the circumstances surrounding Sarah's family bereavements, which were a long-standing topic of village gossip.

The wedded bliss the couple portrayed was little more than a sham and as the weeks progressed William was seen drinking in the Chequers Inn, Wrestlingworth. He was often alone and the drinking sessions became more and more frequent. Everyone knew that something was troubling him, for it was out of character for him to behave in such a manner. William would not confide in anyone, he kept his marital problems to himself – sadly, his wife could not do so.

One Saturday evening William returned home from the village inn and a violent quarrel ensued as his wife demanded to know where he had been. Sarah scolded her husband for drinking so much, William declined to get involved, but Sarah was livid and continued to rant and rave until William could take no more. In a brief moment of despair he lashed out at his wife. It was to be an action which he would regret for the short time he had left to live.

The following day Sarah met with one of her supposed lovers, William Waldock, a local man. She told Waldock about her husband and how he was continually ill treating

The cottage at Wrestlingworth where William Dazley was poisoned by his wife Sarah in 1842.

her, adding that she 'would do for anyone who hits her'. The insecure woman then proceeded to tell another neighbour a similar tale in a bid to gain sympathy and to poison people's minds against her husband. The good people of Wrestlingworth realised that there were two sides to every tale, and the stories told by Sarah were, in the main, ignored.

A few days after this incident William Dazley was taken seriously ill, vomiting and complaining of wretched stomach pains. Doctor Sandell from Potton was called and duly carried out a thorough examination, pills were prescribed and almost immediately William began to recover.

Within a few days William was on the mend although still bedridden. Ann Mead was busying herself in the kitchen of the small house when Sarah, who was unaware of Ann's presence, came in. The young girl stood quietly and was amazed to see Sarah begin to roll her own pills! It did not mean a great deal to her at the time, she found it more curious than anything else, believing that Sarah was making the pills to sweeten the taste of those prescribed by the doctor.

Later that same day Sarah visited one of her friends, Mrs Carver in Potton. She told Mrs Carver that she was worried about her husband's health (she did not explain that he was getting better) and that she was going to visit Doctor Sandell for more pills. Mrs Carver offered her kindest regards to William and Sarah left. A few minutes later Mrs Carver saw Sarah walking back towards Wrestlingworth. She was within a few feet of her when she saw Sarah throw some pills into a hedgerow, seemingly replacing these in the container with some others. Mrs Carver called out to Sarah that she had dropped some pills, but Sarah replied that she had little faith in Doctor Sandell's medication and she had visited the village healer, Mrs Gurr, who had provided a different remedy.

At home Sarah offered the pills to her husband, who at

once noticed a difference between these and the ones given to him by Doctor Sandell. He refused to take them. Ann Mead became involved; she had been nursing William and a good trusting relationship had been forged between them. Ann persuaded William to take the pills by taking one herself, and William consumed the medication proffered by his wife. In consequence of this both Ann and William fell violently ill, once again with severe stomach pains and vomiting. William Dazley rushed out of the house and into the rear yard, desperate to gulp in quantities of fresh air. He vomited on the ground by the pig pen and returned indoors. Unwittingly the vomit was eagerly lapped up by one of the greedy pigs in the yard; the sad beast was found dead the following morning!

Both William and Ann survived the sickness, which was most mysterious, and amazingly neither suspected Sarah of any nefarious actions. Sarah was now desperate. She continued to feed her husband more and more pills in greater dosages and reassured him that the pills were from Doctor Sandell. William Dazley died on 30th October 1842. The subsequent inquest was a farce. No suspicious circumstances were deemed to surround the death, which was ascribed to an infection. William was buried in Wrestlingworth churchyard.

At the tender age of 23, Sarah Dazley had twice been widowed. For most people such tragedies would be catastrophic and cause long term grief, but Sarah Dazley was not your average human being. Indeed, Sarah typified evil. Within a few weeks of William Dazley's death she had taken up an open relationship with William Waldock. It was not that Waldock attempted to force himself upon her, indeed it was the opposite. Once again Sarah's strong personality dictated the future of the relationship and within a few weeks the couple announced their engagement to be married.

Amongst the inquisitive villagers of Wrestlingworth the

general consensus of opinion was that Sarah had had something to do with William Dazley's death. Peer pressure was placed upon William Waldock to sever his relationship with Sarah and various facts were pointed out to him, including her promiscuity. He duly broke off the engagement, electing to refrain from seeing her any more. Some of the villagers decided to inform the local coroner, Mr Eagles, of their suspicions, and the official listened intently and agreed to reinvestigate the deaths of Simeon Mead, his child and William Dazley. This would either clear Sarah Dazley of suspicion or prove her guilt. He ordered that the body of William Dazley be exhumed and a further post mortem held.

On Monday, 20th March 1843 an inquest was held in the Chequers Inn, Wrestlingworth. It was announced that William Dazley's body contained lethal traces of poison; white arsenic had been found in his intestines. The death was confirmed to be under suspicious circumstances and a warrant for Sarah's arrest issued. However, that cunning young woman knew that all was about to be revealed and she took off, searching for sanctuary in London. Superintendent Blunden of Biggleswade made a few discreet enquiries within the district and ascertained Sarah's precise whereabouts. Arriving in Upper Wharf Street, London, he found Sarah and effected an arrest. She told him that she was aware of the vicious rumours emanating from Potton and Wrestlingworth about her killing her husbands, but they were not true. The evil woman proclaimed that she was innocent until proven guilty and that the authorities would find it impossible to prove her guilt, as she had no knowledge of poisons and had never procured any other than official medication prescribed by Doctor Sandell. She calmly stated, 'I was on my way to Bedford to give myself up, I am innocent.'

The rooms of her London lodgings were searched but revealed very little in the way of evidence. The return trip to

Bedford was carried out in two stages, the prisoner and her captors staying overnight at the Swan Inn, Biggleswade, where Sarah spent a sleepless night, constantly asking her travel companions questions upon executions and trials.

Meanwhile the authorities had begun to investigate every facet of the case, and the bodies of Simeon Mead and his child were exhumed and examined. Positive signs of poison in the young child were found but insufficient evidence existed to prove that Simeon Mead had died by similar means.

Sarah had begun to plot and scheme. She told the authorities that her first husband and child had been poisoned by none other than William Dazley, who wanted rid of them so he could have her all to himself. She further claimed that once she knew of this she poisoned Dazley, handing out her own form of retribution. An ingenious story but one which was filled with inconsistencies and no-one believed her. The fact that she was suspected of the murder of her own innocent and helpless baby manufactured great public hatred towards her.

The trial of Sarah Dazley commenced at Bedford in July 1843. Her defence counsel, Mr O'Malley explained that she had administered the poison to her husband, William Dazley by mistake, a total contradiction of what she told the investigating authorities. It was her final attempt to twist the truth to her own benefit. The court did not examine the murder of the young baby, since sufficient evidence existed to prove Sarah Dazley's guilt in murdering her husband and such guilt would indicate that the baby died by the same callous hand. The case offered by the defence began to crumble, not through any fault of Mr O'Malley, but through the lies Sarah had told him. First, two chemists came forward and gave evidence that they had sold arsenic to Sarah Dazley a short time before William Dazley had passed away, while Mrs Carver told of the episode she had witnessed with the pills. William Waldock was called to confirm that on 13th October 1842, Sarah and William Dazley had a violent verbal altercation. He told the court that Sarah had said to him, 'He struck me, I'll be damned if I don't do for any man that ever hits me.' The evidence against Sarah Dazley was overwhelming.

The jury retired, only to return just 30 minutes later with a verdict of 'guilty of murder'. The judge, Baron Alderson found himself angered whilst passing sentence upon Sarah; he commented that it was a sin to murder a man she supposedly cherished, but to take the life of a young innocent child was utterly heartless. He could not sufficiently express his anguish over such an atrocious deed and recommended that she should ask for the mercy of her Redeemer. He then sentenced Sarah to death and instructed that she should be returned to Bedford prison until such time as the sentence was carried out.

It is said that whilst incarcerated in prison, Sarah taught herself to read and write. She took to reading the Bible and begged her Maker for mercy each evening. She refused to talk with other prisoners and was very much a loner. The execution date had been set for Sunday 5th August 1843 and she therefore had very little time to fret over her situation. She would sit for hour after hour staring into space and sobbing aloud, and she found it difficult to eat as the fateful day grew closer. News of her grief quickly spread throughout the town and this suffering amazingly aroused great sympathy. Indeed, so great was this sympathy that the authorities were forced to place an extra guard on her cell door as it was believed that some citizens of the town were plotting her escape.

The day of the execution soon arrived, when a crowd of some 12,000 assembled to witness Sarah Dazley's last few minutes on this earth. It was the first execution to take place in Bedford since 1833. A buzz of excitement ran through the crowd as the minute of the execution neared; among those gathered was William Waldock who, unlike most people there, stood in silence. It is impossible to understand what emotions must have been running through his mind as he watched his ex-fiancee executed.

A stage had been erected upon which stood the gallows. The executioner, William Calcraft stood awaiting the arrival of Sarah Dazley, who was brought up from the condemned cell. The prison governor asked if she had anything to say prior to being 'turned off'. She declined the offer to confess her sins but asked that Calcraft be swift in his operation. He pinioned her hands in front of her, which was seen by the assembled throng as the time to fall silent. The officials withdrew from the platform, Calcraft made one or two slight adjustments and turned her to face away from the crowd. The signal was given and the bolt was withdrawn, plunging Sarah Dazley through the platform, suspended by the executioner's rope. Dazley died almost immediately.

THE KILLING
OF PC SNOW

IN 1868 the village of Benington, to the east of Stevenage, was fortunate enough to be provided with the services of a keen police constable by the name of Benjamin Snow. The task of a village constable is not an easy one in any circumstances, let alone in the Victorian era, but Snow was blessed with a great deal of commonsense. A family man, he was married with three children. In such a job, a constable requires the respect of a community and respect is what Snow earned himself; apart from those who frequently met him in his professional capacity, almost everyone had a good word to say about the officer. The greatest task Benjamin Snow faced was combatting the classic country crime of poaching, local farmers and livestock owners having been plagued for years by such activities.

Over the following two to three years Snow fought a constant battle with the poachers and one has to say that he had a fair amount of success. None of those with whom he dealt hailed from Benington, they came from other villages and over the period Snow got to know most of them by sight and by the various methods they used. Perhaps the most prolific local poacher and criminal within the district during this period was John Chapman, who was described as a rugged, foul-mouthed man complete with whiskers!

A warrant for Chapman's arrest had been in existence since 1865 and was held at Stevenage. He was a slippery customer who tended to carry out his crimes in a variety of places, hence when PC Snow heard that the notorious Chapman was believed to be in his area he was only too keen to apprehend him. It was Tuesday, 10th January 1871 and Snow obtained the assistance of two other local village constables, Williams and Worby, as an operation was planned to locate and arrest Chapman. The three police officers elected to visit all local farmers and search barns and exposed outbuildings in their quest to find their quarry.

Before leaving his home for duty on that day, Snow told his wife that he believed that Chapman was back in his beat area after a stay in London. His wife warned him to be careful and Snow left home for a meeting at nearby Sacombe Pound. For some inexplicable reason he forgot to take his truncheon with him, a matter which he was to greatly regret. As he walked through the village he was told by a villager that Chapman was in Benington, and Snow prepared himself to give chase once he could locate the criminal.

Meanwhile, Chapman was walking in Cutting Lane when he was met by a local man who bade him a good day and asked how he was. Chapman made an angry response to this insincere remark and continued upon his way. Very shortly he was joined by an impressionable young man by the name of James Gilbey, who had heard the tales of Chapman and was somewhat in awe of his new-found acquaintance. Gilbey walked into the village with Chapman but after a short while Chapman told Gilbey to remain where he was as he had some business to do elsewhere, a man to meet on a personal matter. Gilbey did as he was instructed. Within a few minutes he heard the report of a gun being fired, a single shot. PC Snow also heard that shot and hurried on through the village.

Chapman rejoined Gilbey and they continued upon their way. Behind them was PC Benjamin Snow and he asked a villager, William Beadle, if he knew who the two persons ahead of him were. Beadle could throw no light on matters, so Snow continued after the pair. A few minutes later he saw the younger of the two men leave the other's company. In fact, Gilbey had been told to go by Chapman, but not before the youngster had pointed out the fast-approaching figure of Benjamin Snow. Chapman, who had fresh blood on his hands, asked Gilbey the directions to Green End.

A few moments later Snow rushed past Gilbey towards Chapman, who was walking away from him. The young man turned to see what happened next. He could sense the volatile atmosphere as Snow neared his man and Gilbey suddenly became frightened, panicked and ran away as fast as his legs would carry him. The last thing he saw of Chapman was PC Snow taking hold of his jacket; he did not wish to see anything else. The villagers of Benington heard another loud crack as the second report of a gun echoed through the village, then there was an eerie silence.

William Beadle, who was still working in his garden, saw Benjamin Snow coming back along the road. He was clutching the left side of his head. A road worker also saw Snow holding his head as though in serious pain; he asked the constable, who still wore his hat, if he had a headache. Snow yelled back, 'I have been shot.' The man noticed blood running down the side of the officer's face close to his left ear.

Within a few minutes Snow was back at his home. His wife hurriedly sent for the local doctor, Mr Hodges of Watton-at-Stone. Her husband was almost insensible, and when asked by his loved one what had happened, he simply replied, 'Enemy, got gun shot, run away.' Poor Mrs Snow was horrified by the wound her husband had received, there was a gaping hole in the side of his head close to the left ear. Snow's condition deteriorated throughout the day and by the time Doctor Hodges returned later the unfortunate policeman was dead.

News was passed to Inspector Reynolds at Stevenage that

The lane at Benington where PC Benjamin Snow was shot in 1871 is still a peaceful and remote spot today.

an assault upon a police officer had occurred in Benington. He at once went to Snow's police house, but alas was too late, the officer had died prior to his arrival. The following morning, Reynolds visited those who had heard or seen anything suspicious on that day, including James Gilbey, but the young man could tell him very little of what had occurred after he left Chapman. Gilbey took Reynolds to where he saw PC Snow take hold of the criminal's jacket. In the mud and dirt the Inspector saw clear signs of a struggle. A sprinkling of snow had fallen on the ground earlier the previous morning and the freezing cold conditions had preserved the scene and the footprints of those present. It was clear that one set of prints belonged to the police officer and the other to his killer; one set was well worn and had been repaired by the use of a few nails. This set of footprints continued to the bottom of the lane where they stopped at a footpath leading to Ardeley. The wearer of the boots walked in a curious manner, his left foot seemed to turn outwards even though it was obvious that he had been running from the scene of the scuffle. Realising that Chapman was the obvious suspect for this heinous act, Reynolds contacted the Metropolitan Police in the belief that the killer might once again return to London as a place of sanctuary.

John Chapman had in fact returned to his lodgings at 1 Goff's Cottages, Nightingale Road, Wood Green, London. Early in the morning of Friday, 15th January 1871, Chapman was asleep in his bed when Police Sergeant Turner of the Metropolitan Police entered his premises, ordering Chapman to dress. The sergeant seized a pair of old boots repaired with nails and informed the suspect that he was under arrest on suspicion of murder; the callous killer retorted, 'I was in Benington, I have nothing further to add on the matter.' A search of the house revealed shot and powder flasks, a gun and a dead duck. The latter had been shot by Chapman shortly after he had met with James Gilbey, the first of the two shots fired in the village that fateful day.

The seized items were handed over to Inspector Reynolds who at once observed that the soles of the boots were identical to the pattern made in the snow at the scene of the crime. Unfortunately, no true comparison could be made as snow had fallen heavily since the murder. Chapman was brought to Stevenage and interviewed by Reynolds who further noticed that the suspect in custody had a curious gait, his left foot leading off to the left as he walked, similar to the footprints he noted in Benington.

Chapman was later conveyed to Hertford where he was placed in the cells in Shire Hall. He was brought back to Benington on Monday, 18th January 1871 for the inquest hearing, which was held at the school house. The 37 year old killer with five children denied everything; he seemed to remain aloof from the hearing going on around him, the loss of human life apparently meaning very little to him. His reply to the charges brought against him was, 'It was not me.' The jury took but a few minutes to return a verdict of 'Wilful Murder', thus committing Chapman to trial at the Hertfordshire Assizes.

PC Snow's grave in Benington churchyard. The funeral was attended by over 40 policemen from the county.

The trial opened in March of the same year before Mr Justice Hannen. The defence counsel raised a point of law which was to cause discussion for several years after the event. It was claimed that as Snow was not in personal possession of the arrest warrant then he had no power to effect a lawful arrest and that any person had a right to defend themselves, resisting arrest until death if necessary.

The case was heard and Hannen was left to his summing up, which some to this day feel was devoid of commonsense. He sided with Chapman's defence counsel, stating that if an individual should be arrested unlawfully or by an unauthorised party then there were reasonable grounds to resist such an arrest; however, it should not be a natural conclusion that such an individual has the right to defend himself to such an extent that it causes the death of another. Should the jury feel that the wound caused to PC Snow was so inflicted, in consequence of his unlawful actions in attempting to arrest Chapman without possession of the warrant, and by the defendant's over-enthusiastic defence of his rights as provoked by the policeman, then he should be found guilty of manslaughter and not murder.

The jury almost immediately returned a verdict of guilty of manslaughter. Chapman was then sentenced to 15 years' penal servitude. It was only when passing this sentence that Hannen discussed the seriousness of the verdict. He added that it should never be thought a correct and proper action that a man should be allowed to kill a police constable who is effecting an arrest without personal possession of a warrant. Yet on this very occasion the foolish Hannen had so justified Snow's murder.

Benjamin Snow was buried at St Peter's churchyard, Benington. There was a large gathering at the funeral which included Colonel Robertson, Chief Constable of Hertfordshire, one superintendent, four inspectors and 40 constables, including Williams and Worby who had assisted Snow in the operation to locate and arrest Chapman.

Benjamin Snow was the second Hertfordshire police officer to be killed on duty; in 1857 the horrifically mutilated body of PC John Starkins was recovered from a pond near Six Hills, Stevenage. His killer was believed to be a local thief and rogue by the name of Jeremiah Carpenter, but despite a mass of circumstantial evidence against him Carpenter was found 'Not Guilty', albeit the jury believed it to be a case of 'great suspicion'. Neither Carpenter nor Chapman received their just rewards for their actions, since to deliberately kill those who are upholding the law can never be condoned.

A MOST
MYSTERIOUS CASE

IN the mid 17th century (around 1645) rumours were rife around the town of Bedford of a stranger who was searching for his wife, believed to have come to the town with another gentleman. The stranger was reported to be offering large sums of money to those who could provide him with information, but, despite the rumours, it seems that no-one ever actually met him.

Town life continued in its normal fashion until the rumours again began to circulate. This time they were a little more troubling. The stranger, it was said, had returned to Bedford and had vowed to avenge himself for his wife's treatment of him. The man was claimed to be an arch villain from London, a murderer no less! The authorities heard of the gossip and at once extra guards were placed in the town in an attempt to deter the stranger from committing any crime. Anyone who appeared a little different was stopped and searched and questioned by the authorities as they desperately attempted to locate this man. For many days the town lived in fear, as further tales spread of the atrocities he had committed elsewhere; some had heard of him torturing his victims before burning them alive, while others said he would sever limbs from the living body before tossing them into the nearest river.

Seventeenth century England was a remarkably naive society and the tales of the stranger continued for several weeks without any tangible substance. The fear instilled throughout the town was similar to that displayed in White-chapel, London, in 1888 during the Jack the Ripper scare – yet nothing had actually transpired in Bedford!

Eventually the rumours dwindled away and the fear dis-appeared – until one market day when an unattended cart which appeared to bear a full load was discovered unclaimed in the corner of the market. The greedy traders peered beneath the covering of the load and were horrified to find what appeared to be huge chunks of a human torso minus its head. The authorities were called but played the incident down; it was claimed that the joints were not human but those of cattle to be sold at the market, yet no cart owner could be found and all those who saw the lumps of meat swore that they were human remains. Despite this the belief grew that the 'stranger' fable was nothing more than vicious gossip.

Some weeks had passed when a man by the name of Sharpe was stopped in the town carrying two great bladed knives. He said he was on his way to Leeds to deliver them to a friend, but he could provide no reasonable purpose for the use of such instruments, which were at once seized. The man remained in Bedford for a short time and stayed at lodgings near Kempston. He was something of an enigma, never giving any information about himself nor telling anyone why he was in the town. Sharpe left Bedford after his brief stay, minus knives, and was never heard or seen of again. However, just a few days later the remains of two bodies were allegedly found beneath a bridge in the town; the bodies had been butchered and had the appearance of having been there for many days. The victims were never identified, nor their killer.

Some believed that it was the mysterious Mr Sharpe who had finally carried out his revenge upon an unfaithful wife and her lover, yet surely his knives had been seized by the

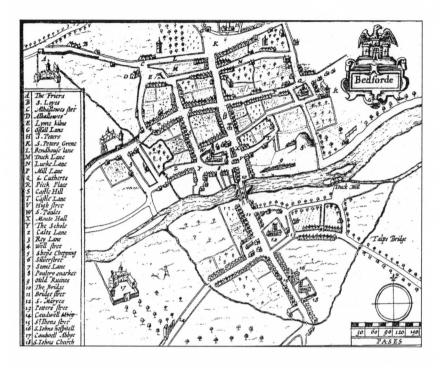

Speed's bird's eye view of Bedford in 1610. Some 30 years later, human remains were found beneath the town bridge.

time the murders occurred? Others believed that the remains were dumped there having been transported from another part of the country where the murders were committed, possibly London, and the coincidence with the mysterious Mr Sharpe was just that. Yet what of the meat/remains found in the cart at the market? Are we to believe that Sharpe or someone else carried out three separate murders in the town? Sadly, we shall never know. The records are sketchy, but there is no trace of any missing persons suspected of being the victims of this crime, and most certainly if they had been inhabitants of Bedford, then someone would have reported them missing after the furore of the grisly find. It seems more likely that the victims were from elsewhere and that Bedford had been used as a dumping ground; even in the 17th century it was most accessible.

As a matter of coincidence, a similar spate of crimes was carried out in London almost a century later. It was believed that the victims were intended for the use of medical students who practised their skills either on preordered corpses or prearranged murdered victims. The likelihood of a similar modus operandi in the Bedford crimes should be considered. But you know what they say, 'Beware of Strangers'!

POISON AT THE ASYLUM

CAROLINE Ansell had been a patient at Leavesden Lunatic Asylum, near Watford, for about 15 months when she received on 9th March 1899 a small parcel addressed to her in Ward Seven. The parcel, which had for security reasons been opened by a senior member of staff, contained a cake, a small flat sandwich cake with a filling which was later described as 'very yellow'. Caroline Ansell was thrilled to receive such a present, which had been sent by her younger sister, Mary Ansell, who was just 22.

The following day the cake was cut and shared among the inmates of Ward Seven; Caroline obviously had the biggest share. Unfortunately the cake tasted very bitter but the majority of it was avidly consumed by Caroline's friends. Within hours of digesting the cake those who had eaten it were violently ill, vomiting and complaining of stomach pains. Twenty four hours later the majority had improved sufficiently to again devour a hearty lunch, all except poor Caroline who remained bedridden. Caroline's condition did improve slightly although she was not her usual buoyant self. Two days later she was transferred to the asylum's infirmary wing where her condition was closely monitored. The stomach pains grew more violent and it was something of a blessing when she lapsed into an unconscious state, a condition from which she was never to recover. Indeed, she died that same evening.

Initially the cause of death was thought to be peritonitis, but the gossip of the nursing staff ensured that rumours were rife recalling how everyone who had eaten the sandwich cake sent by Mary Ansell had fallen ill. Eventually a post-mortem was carried out resulting in the confirmation that Caroline Ansell had died by virtue of phosphorous poisoning, the traces of which had been found within the dead girl's abdomen. It seemed clear that the authorities were now about to report that someone had deliberately murdered Caroline Ansell.

Superintendent Wood commenced enquiries at the asylum along with Constable Piggott. Staff recalled how on 22nd February that same year, Caroline had received another parcel from her sister which contained tea and sugar; this had been thrown out as it had a bitter taste. PC Piggott searched through the asylum's refuse and located a brown paper wrapper addressed to Caroline, which bore a WC1 postmark.

The police were now faced with a difficult problem; there was immediate suspicion of Mary Ansell, but why should she wish to kill her sister? There was at this stage little or no motive.

It was confirmed that Mary Ansell resided in Tankerton Street (off Grays Inn Road) where she worked as a maid-servant. This was a WC1 address, as too was her employer's in Great Coram Street, which is now known as Coram Street. Detailed but discreet enquiries were made at various addresses in this area and it was soon ascertained that in September 1898 Mary Ansell had taken out life insurance on her sister Caroline. The agreement had been drawn up with the Royal London Friendly Society who had an agent who called at Mr and Mrs Patrick Maloney's residence in Great Coram Street (Mary's employer). Mary had improvised her application by stating that her sister was a maidservant at the asylum rather than an inmate, and she further fraudulently claimed that Caroline was in good health. John Cooper, the agent accepted Mary's claims and duly allowed her to sign the form, without first making enquiries; perhaps this was because the Maloneys were such good and valued customers, we shall never know, but what is obvious is that Cooper was remarkably stupid to accept the word of Mary Ansell alone.

The policy was for a total of £22 10s 0d, insuring Caroline's life. However, as a claim had been submitted within six months of the agreement being drawn up, the insurance company agreed to pay out just half of the insured amount, £11 5s 0d, which although a remarkably low sum would be sufficient to keep Mary Ansell satisfied for a reasonable time. The police were still not happy that murder would occur for such a paltry sum but further investigation into Mary Ansell's background was to prove damning.

Mary was engaged to be married that same year and a provisional date had been set for Easter 1899. However the cost of a wedding, then as now, was immense, and her boy-friend had decided that it would be better to wait until they could raise sufficient funds to get married and set up a respectable family home which he could afford to maintain. This decision had caused Mary much grief, she was devastated by the news and the fear of losing her boyfriend was so great that it seemed likely that this was why she hatched a plot to kill. The police had sufficient cause to arrest her and duly did so without further delay, though Mary denied any such involvement and claimed that she loved her sister, 'it was all a big mistake'.

The only mistake had been made by her and the police knew it. A search of her sleeping area revealed further incriminating evidence when a small jar containing phos-phorous paste (rat-poison) was found; it was a popular brand which was readily available around town. The Maloneys were interviewed and could never recall requesting that such an item should be purchased, as far as they were concerned they had no problems with vermin. It was not too long before the owner of a hardware shop in Marchmont Street advised the police that he recalled Mary Ansell visiting his shop in either February or March 1899. The visits were recalled as Mary had actually purchased several jars of the poison, claiming it was required to rid the Maloney house of rats!

Mary Ansell was brought to trial at Hertford Assizes on 29th June 1899. The evidence for the prosecution was so precise and clear cut that they had all but finished their case halfway through the first day of the trial. Quite unexpectedly, Mary's parents were called to the witness stand to give evidence. Her father explained that Mary was adamant that he should not allow the authorities to carry out a post-mortem on Caroline's remains; he thought that this was because the two sisters were on close terms and Mary could not bear the thought of Caroline's body being so desecrated. Mary Ansell took the witness stand and denied sending both parcels; she had no cause to send tea and sugar nor a cake to her sister, and she had not seen nor communicated with Caroline since December 1897. The prosecution mentioned a letter which had been sent to Caroline, allegedly from a cousin, stating that both her (Caroline's) parents had died. Mary again denied writing or sending such a letter, despite the fact that a handwriting expert had confirmed the writing to be very similar to hers. In an attempt to cover her tracks Mary admitted purchasing the poison to kill the rats but would confess to nothing more, after all, she claimed, 'I am innocent of any crime.' Mary was then questioned as to how and why she took out insurance on her sister's life. She claimed that Mr Cooper had forced her into doing so, after she had told him of her follies and how she hoped one day to give Caroline a decent funeral.

Her defence counsel could do little to destroy the prosecution's case, in truth he appears to have been somewhat

After Mary Ansell's trial, newspapers were in the forefront of the campaign to have the death sentence commuted. The Home Secretary remained firm however and she was hanged at St Albans prison in 1899.

dilatory with his investigations and in his cross-examination of witnesses. It was no real surprise when the jury returned a verdict of 'Guilty of murder'. More courtroom drama occurred as the judge was passing sentence, when a shrill scream echoed through the court chambers. It was Mary Ansell's mother, anxious and desperate as her own flesh and blood stood, defenceless and almost forlornly, in the shadow of the gallows.

Amazingly there was a great deal of sympathy for Mary, undoubtedly a cold-blooded killer. The verdict, or her guilt, was never in question, but there was strong public opinion that execution was too extreme a punishment for her actions.

It was a well established belief that Mary Ansell herself was insane. Newspapers demanded that an appeal should be arranged and the death penalty commuted to a term of imprisonment; one enterprising journalist even attempted to claim that insanity ran in the Ansell family, albeit both her parents seemed perfectly sane.

Another newspaper located Mary's boyfriend, who had not been called to give evidence. He told reporters that Mary had been keen to be married and had attempted to pressurise him into doing so. She was extremely insecure and believed that her parents had been oppressing her for most of her life. Finally in a last ditch attempt to force him into marriage she had bought several items of furniture for their future home and had told friends that the wedding was imminent; sadly she never discussed such arrangements with her boyfriend. He added that on one occasion Mary had met him wearing a new dress, which she told him was to be her wedding dress. At this stage the unfortunate young man had not proposed to her nor discussed anything vaguely relevant to marriage.

Mrs Maloney, one of her employers, was another to suffer the attentions of enthusiastic reporters. She stated that it was always her belief that Mary was of a weak state of mind and seemingly immature, and her condition had grown worse as time progressed. One pertinent comment seems to sum Mary Ansell up, 'Vacant'.

It was claimed within the pages of the *Daily Mail*, which was the main instigator in attempting to have the death penalty in this case quashed, that insanity had been found on both sides of the Ansell family, and the campaign on Mary's behalf began to increase in pace and effort. Unfortunately, and to this day it is still the salient point of the case, the simple fact that Mary Ansell murdered her sister with malice aforethought is irrefutable. Her state of mind at the time was such that she could hold down a reasonable job with some responsibility and carry out the initial commission of the crime without attracting attention. Her cowardly act caused her own sister to die an agonising death.

The authorities eventually gave in to the media pressure and consented to a review of the case and Mary's frame of mind at the time, but the decision was not reversed and no reprieve was granted. The *Daily Mail* claimed to have received somewhere in the region of 10,000 letters protesting against the decision. Various small committees were formed in an attempt to stop the execution and one group even sent a telegram to Her Majesty Queen Victoria, but still the Home Secretary stood by his decision. Mary Ansell was to hang.

On Wednesday, 19th July 1899 at St Albans prison, Mary Ansell met with James Billington, her executioner. At precisely 8 am Billington carried out his duty in a professional manner as Ansell fell seven feet through the drop, causing instantaneous death. Her remains were buried in the corner of St Albans prison set aside for such burials. Just 31 years later when the prison was partially demolished, the remains of Mary Ansell and two other persons executed at the prison were exhumed and reinterred in St Albans cemetery, where they still lie.

Murder is an awful crime, and the planning and scheming undertaken by the killer can make it seem all the more gruesome. In this case Mary Ansell murdered a defenceless woman who had done her no harm, nor was she likely to. Perhaps the realisation of what she had done later affected her mental state, but she undoubtedly knew what she was doing at the time.

THE KILLER
OF DUNSTABLE

THE peaceful village of Elstow is situated just off the busy A6 London to Carlisle trunk road. It was the birthplace in the 17th century of the renowned John Bunyan, who spent much of his childhood and adolescent years here. The surrounding countryside, however, is perhaps more synonymous with a much more sinister character than the great Bunyan, an individual whose reputation is almost legendary, though over 900 years have passed since he struck terror into the heart of the Bedfordshire countryside. His name was Thomas Dun.

Thomas Dun was born in the 11th century in a small holding close to the village of Elstow, though its precise location has never been ascertained. As a youngster he was extremely envious of others and their possessions, and would regularly steal from family and friends. By the time he had matured in age but not character, Dun had acquired expensive tastes and habits and thieving had become second nature, as too had the use of violence and deception. It is claimed that Dun would often dress in disguise; for example, he once placed false limbs on his body in an attempt to play an invalided beggar. Once he had aroused attention he would suddenly leap upon his quarry and steal from them, using any form of violence he deemed necessary. Human life meant very little to Dun, especially the expendable life of another, to him the only objective in his own small world was power obtained by wealth.

Such was the case when one day Dun was walking in the country lanes close to Bedford and saw a waggoner driving a horse-drawn cart loaded with corn. He immediately approached the cart, which was heading in the direction of Bedford, and caused it to stop. The waggoner alighted and on doing so was set about by Dun who swiftly stabbed him twice, killing him instantly.

Not content with this horrendous act, Dun then proceeded to dig a grave using the unfortunate waggoner's own spade. The calculating Dun then buried his victim and duly drove the cart and load into Bedford where he sold it lock, stock and barrel. Armed with the ill-gotten gains of his nefarious activities, he squandered the lot.

For some time he elected to work the highway alone, presumably feeling that this reduced the chances of being caught during the commission of a crime, and with no-one else knowing of his activities he could rest knowing that others could not discuss his current whereabouts. The arrogant Dun, however, had failed to appreciate one factor. The highways were not exactly the safest place to earn one's living, and even highwaymen occasionally suffered attacks from other rogues. One suspects that his contemporaries must have harboured grievances towards him, because personal threats began to reach his ears. With this in mind, Dun took to the dense woodland of the country in an attempt to disappear for a while.

Dun realised that he could no longer run the risk of working alone, he needed fools to carry out crimes on his behalf. It was not too long before he accumulated a large gang of rogues who displayed loyalty among their own but disregard for outsiders. The years which followed saw the activities of Thomas Dun and his gang increase to the extent that many would travel miles out of their way in order to avoid passing directly through Bedfordshire. The Dun gang

The church and moot hall at Elstow. This peaceful village was the birthplace of two very different men, the great writer John Bunyan, and the villainous highwayman Thomas Dun.

operated most successfully on the road between Towcester and St Albans which was one of the main routes through the county, and various travellers met their end on this stretch of highway as Dun collected their personal treasures and riches.

The national outrage caused by the crimes soon reached the ears of King Henry I and there is a story that he ordered that a town be built, Dunstable, to act as a staging post along the highway and provide a sanctuary for travellers. The building of the town, however, failed to deter Dun and his gang.

It can have come as no real surprise when Dun heard the news that the Sheriff of Bedford and a number of his men were scouring the countryside for the gang and in particular, their mentor. Dun saw this as a challenge and with great cunning changed location to an exceptionally dense part of the woodland which provided ideal cover. With his base camp set, Dun then sent out a number of his men to identify how many of the Sheriff's men were in the vicinity. It was not too long before he ascertained that his gang far outnumbered the authorities.

Dun mustered his men and confronted their prey. Eleven of the Sheriff's men were taken prisoner and duly executed, their bodies left hanging, naked, from the boughs of woodland trees. The fine uniform they wore was seized and was to be put to good use in the committing of further criminal offences.

The gang swiftly moved on and wearing the top coats seized from the Sheriff's men they visited a castle (one of many fortified houses of the time which are no longer in evidence). The group approached the guards and requested that the drawbridge be lowered in order that they could enter on the direct order of His Majesty King Henry I; they informed the guards that they were searching for Thomas Dun and his gang who were believed to be in the area. The drawbridge was lowered and the gang entered the castle. Thomas Dun continued to act out his role as a lawful agent with great enthusiasm and conviction. His men searched the castle grounds looking for any valuables which they could steal, and so this charade continued, with the lord of the castle believing that he was in the presence of the Sheriff's men. After a time Dun ordered that great trunks held in the lord's private chambers should be opened in case they harboured any of the Dun gang. The keys were brought and the trunks opened, and the gang then stole all items of value before retreating to their woodland hideout without further challenge.

News of the theft from the trunks reached the lord of the castle, who until that time had attempted to assist in every manner. Quite naturally he was disturbed that such an atrocious act should take place, and he at once addressed the King and Parliament who ordered an investigation into the matter. What is quite amazing about this whole incident is the fact that everyone seemingly accepted that this act had been carried out by actual officials from the Sheriff's office! One by one the Sheriff's men were interviewed about the incident, and all truthfully denied any knowledge of the affair. However, pressures from the highest in the land insisted that those guilty should be executed, hence the Bedford authorities were forced to take rather drastic action. With every Sheriff's officer denying the charges put to them it was decided to execute one of them in an attempt to instil fear among the offending few who would, it was hoped, be identified by innocents fearing for their own lives. It never worked. The decomposing bodies of the eleven Sheriff's men ambushed and executed by Dun's gang were discovered, and it was then that the authorities realised the error of their ways and that a deception had taken place. The Dun gang had pulled off their greatest crime yet, and Dun was still at large with little clue as to his whereabouts!

Dun had in fact left his men in Bedfordshire, where he realised that his life was in greater danger after this latest outrage than ever before, and had removed himself, heavily disguised, to Yorkshire where he at once recommenced his criminal acts for a while before realising that the rewards were greater in his home county.

On his return Dun once again rallied his men and set forth on a huge criminal campaign. The gang worked well. However, the burden of such responsibility bore heavily on the shoulders of the leader, who preferred solitude and seemingly felt restricted and suffocated by the tight-knit community of the group which now numbered about 50.

It was this which created Dun's greatest weakness, for whilst he enjoyed his moments of solitude rambling through the country lanes of the county, he was vulnerable. Perhaps his arrogance had blinded him to the dangers such singular freedom offered, for the authorities were desperate to apprehend him and had consistently maintained their search for him.

Whilst alone, Dun one day ventured into Dunstable, flaunting his confidence and teasing the authorities. He had various safe houses which he could visit if necessary and one can almost perceive that he felt invincible; this is no wonder as the period of time over which he had carried out these outrages was considerable indeed! Unaware that half a dozen of the Sheriff's men had been alerted by informants of his presence within Dunstable, he visited various hostelries, all the time being monitored by the authorities. Suddenly Dun realised that something out of the ordinary was taking place. He took to his heels and frantically fled through the town, finally taking refuge in a safe house, as the authorities, assisted by several dozen citizens, scoured the streets in search of him. The battle of good against evil took a turn the correct way for once, as news of Dun's whereabouts reached the Sheriff's men, who raced to the house. Within minutes a large crowd had assembled in the street.

The authorities did not want to make any mistakes this time and so two armed guards were placed at the threshold of the property. There was no other route of escape available to Dun; England's most wanted criminal was cornered. The assembled throng outside screamed for Dun's blood and the atmosphere was volatile as the crowd sensed that an arrest was imminent. Suddenly, Thomas Dun appeared at the door. The crowd fell silent. Dun, too, stood in silence and it appeared that he was about to throw himself on the mercy of the rabble, then without further warning, he drew a dagger from his clothing and killed one of the guards on duty at the door. Before the second guard could do anything he too had been slain. The crowd stood stunned by what they had just witnessed, as Dun ran straight through them without hindrance, bridled a horse and attempted to ride off. By this stage a wave of anger had swept through the crowd of about 150, many of whom were brandishing sticks, forks, rakes and stones. As Dun rode off the incensed crowd closed in on his horse, causing it to stop in its tracks. Dun was pulled from the horse and one would imagine that this would be the end of the matter – not so! Dun was not yet ready to surrender his liberty to the masses. He drew his sword and flaying it around him, managed to clear immediate space for himself. Then he forced his way through the crowd in a most remarkable manner.

As Dun attempted to make his escape from the town the crowd regrouped, and one can only assume that this was done under the instructions of the Sheriff's officers. Once again they gave chase, which greatly resembled a pack of hounds chasing their quarry, a sly old fox! Dun ran for cover in a field of standing corn and created a small gap between himself and the pack. As he lay in hiding he perhaps once again felt fairly confident that he would escape, having beaten off the worst of the attack, but before he knew it his pursuers, who now numbered about 300, had closed in on him, the majority desperate to tear him limb from limb. Repeating his method of escape, Dun again took up his sword and fled, the crowd forced back by the action of the sharp blade.

Once again a chase ensued, though this time Dun was tiring and the pack were immediately behind him. Within a few hundred yards he came to a river and, quickly removing unnecessary clothing, dived head first into the water, allegedly clenching the blade of the sword between his teeth! He swam to the sanctuary of a small island in the middle of the river but, allowing their quarry no time to rest, his pursuers took out boats and chased after him. As the men approached, Dun fought for his life and managed to severely wound some of his attackers before taking to the water again. He swam off but was quickly surrounded on the water's edge by dozens of men, all armed with sticks and forcing him to remain in the water as others approached in boats. Thomas Dun was surrounded and, as he stood flailing about in the water threatening the authorities with their lives, the first blow struck him on the head and signalled a barrage of blows from all directions, until eventually, senseless, he was dragged from the water. There was great rejoicing as the news of his detention spread. Many felt that he would have been finished off by the crowds, but the English have always been a sporting bunch and quite simply took Dun to a local surgeon who dressed and treated his wounds; he was then taken to Bedford gaol.

Many of the country's leading men visited Dun in order to satisfy their curiosity as to what the man looked like. There was a belief that some killers took the appearance of the Devil, or were markedly different from the average person, but most of those who did visit Dun found him to be simply an arrogant and unrepentant fool.

Two weeks after his detention, Dun was brought from the gaol and into the Bedford market place where a platform had been erected upon which stood the block. Two executioners stood solemnly on the platform, flanking the prisoner. Defiantly, Dun screamed abuse at the crowd and his captors, threatening that.they would never get away with killing him, but his reign of terror was over and no-one now feared him.

The two executioners closed in on their subject. Dun struggled frantically, realising that he had but a few moments left on this earth. He spat and kicked out at his captors, but was overpowered and forced into a kneeling position. Thomas Dun then suffered a barbaric death. First, both of his hands were chopped off at their wrists, his arms were then cut off at the elbow, then at the shoulders. Next off came his feet beneath the ankles, then his legs at the knee, swiftly followed by his thighs which were severed five inches below his trunk. Finally his head was removed. Twelve body pieces were strategically positioned in principal locations within Bedford town in order to remind those who may have been foolish enough to emulate Dun just what punishment awaited them.

Over the months which followed several members of Dun's gang were captured and executed, but to this day no-one can be certain just how many victims there were of the atrocities of Thomas Dun.

POOR OLD
PIGSTICKER

GOING back just a few decades to the 1930s, transient populations were cropping up all over Hertfordshire, Buckinghamshire and so on. One could not call these persons travellers, for they were more static, residing in huts and under canvas as they searched for any source of employment, mostly of the illegal kind. Every so often the railway would take on a number of their sort to carry out hard manual labour, the rewards for this work wasted upon the evils of drink.

One such site was created between Watford and Barnet, close to the bypass road. It had started with a few huts then slowly increased in size as others moved in. There were no flower-lined avenues here, just filth and depravity, rubbish strewn all over the area. Not surprisingly, those who lived in such an environment had little ambition or self respect; it was a matter of survival of the fittest and to these people this meant stealing from friends and neighbours and committing a high percentage of house burglaries in the residential area nearby. Though often caught by the police, they commonly used aliases and the legal system found it difficult to prosecute in a court of law.

It was on the first day of June 1931 that murder visited this human cess-pit. An inhabitant by the name of McGlade happened to be walking past a recently burnt pile of rubbish which was still smouldering, when suddenly he stopped. He thought he had seen a human hand protruding out of the rubbish. He went back and had his fears confirmed. McGlade was a slightly more intelligent member of the dwellers and made contact with the police; he knew that they would have to be involved and he had nothing to hide.

The body was removed from the rubbish and examined by pathologist Sir Bernard Spilsbury who confirmed that the victim was male and had been dead for some time, around three days. The cause of death was a severe blow to the head, fracturing the skull; the body was so badly burned that formal identification was all but impossible. The only clue was a tattoo which was on the back of one hand, a red heart with a sword running through it.

One of the inhabitants of the site recognised the tattoo and declared that the remains were those of Herbert William Ayres, known as 'Pigsticker' to his friends. The police investigation, led by Detective Inspector Bennett, would

Policemen and squad car from the 1930s, the period of the violent death of William 'Pigsticker' Ayres.

have to go no farther than the site itself. Further information came from a man known as John Armstrong who had only recently moved onto the site and was living with two men, Oliver Newman (alias Tiggy) and William Shelly (alias Moosh). Three nights earlier he had been asleep in the men's hut when he was awakened by a disturbance. He had looked up to see Moosh and Tiggy beating Pigsticker over the head. The next thing he knew was that the men were carrying Pigsticker out to the rubbish tip. Armstrong had remained silent as he wanted nothing to do with the sordid affair, and after informing the police he duly disappeared for his own safety.

Newman and Shelly were arrested and questioned at length. They confessed to hitting Ayres over the head with the blunt edge of an axe; this was later found within their hut and matched the depression in Ayres' skull. The reason that they had killed him was that Ayres was suspected of stealing from the hut; a few days prior to his death he had been caught in their hut taking tea and sugar and the two men had beaten him up and warned him not to return. Later, on the day of the crime, some bacon and bread had disappeared, Ayres was at once suspected and duly murdered during the fracas which followed.

Newman and Shelly were tried at the Old Bailey, where they gave their ages as 61 and 57 respectively. The trial lasted just two days and both men were found guilty and sentenced to death. Upon hearing this Shelly commented, 'It has come 20 years too late, still better late than never.'

There are those who believe that John Armstrong was the real thief. It was proved in court that he had removed other items from the hut, and could have taken the bacon and the bread, so Tiggy and Moosh may well have killed a man innocent of the accusations they made against him. If so it is no wonder that Armstrong disappeared so swiftly after the affair!

DOMESTIC MATTERS

TODAY, domestic disputes form a fair percentage of the normal general duties of a patrol policeman. Yet, although the quantity of domestic disputes the police officer of today's force attends has increased, the majority are not what one could call life threatening. This is where the situation has altered over the years; the Victorian police officer must have detested attending such disputes for they could usually expect to find someone with serious injuries, or even become the victim of serious assault themselves.

Tilbrook is now part of Cambridgeshire, but in 1881 it was within the county boundaries of Bedfordshire, located to the north of the county off the A45 and B660. The village itself has hardly changed, and one can still see the old barns and buildings from that era and beyond.

On the 8th November 1881, Police Sergeant Clark was sitting quietly working at his desk in one of the local village police stations when he was called to attend Tilbrook, where a domestic dispute was occurring. Hurriedly the sergeant made his way to the village and was greeted by a crowd of onlookers, all staring at one particular house, that of the Haines family.

Thomas Haines, a corporal in the Royal Engineers, came rushing out to greet Clark, and pointed within. He was pale-looking and speechless, and the sergeant must have wondered what awaited him within the four walls of the tiny house. As he entered the living area he was met by 25 year old Jane Haines who informed the sergeant that she had just got her child to sleep upstairs. Thomas Haines thrust his arm towards the bemused officer and pointed towards the stairs, gesticulating that he should go upstairs and check. Clark was concerned that something extraordinary had occurred but he could not ascertain what it was. Ascending the steep little staircase he reached the main bedroom where he saw the young child asleep on the bed. Gently he approached what he thought was a slumbering baby. It suddenly dawned on him that the child and the bedclothes were covered in blood. Frantically he wiped the blood away from the face and neck of the helpless infant; there he saw a single slit across its throat. Horrified and angry he rushed downstairs and asked what had happened.

Jane Haines openly confessed to taking the child upstairs, laying it on the bed and cutting its throat. Clark called for a doctor and it was not long before Mr Bell arrived on the scene and duly declared the child dead. Jane Haines was arrested for the deliberate murder of her own child. Clark asked what she had used to cut the infant's throat; silently

Bedford Gaol as it looked in about 1820.

Jane Haines walked over to a work basket and removed a cut throat razor. As she handed it to him she stated, 'This is the razor I used to cut the child's throat. I don't know whatever made me do it, I think the Devil must have got hold of me. It was a dear little thing, I did love it.'

Jane Haines was held at Bedford gaol until her trial which commenced on Monday, 16th January 1882. It was clear from the outset that Mrs Haines was not of a sound mind, yet she had been a good and loving wife and mother. Friends and neighbours testified that the woman did not have an ounce of malice in her, yet since the birth of her child she had altered so drastically that she was almost unapproachable. On one occasion she had tried to drown herself and there was a suggestion that she had more than once attempted to steal her husband's gun in order to shoot herself. The jury could give but one verdict on this unfortunate affair; 'not guilty to murder on the grounds of insanity'. Jane Haines was, however, held in custody at Her Majesty's pleasure.

The Victorians had no real understanding of the consequences of post natal depression, which in this instance was quite clearly the problem which sent Jane Haines over the top, causing her to act in a most uncharacteristic manner. Her husband could never have known just how serious the hormone-related problem was, and one can only feel saddened for all concerned.

Our second case based on domestic matters relates to an incident which took place in 1882 in the sleepy village of Heath and Reach, also in Bedfordshire. Mr and Mrs George Battams were known as a jolly old couple; he was 65 years old, his wife 63 years of age. The couple seemed outwardly content enough, they had one son who had started a family of his own, and were simply enjoying the latter years of their life alone, or at the very least, they should have been. The 'real' George Battams, however, was a cantankerous old fool, who regularly verbally abused his wife.

Battams took ill in the latter part of November 1881. He was suffering from severe headaches and found it difficult to work or concentrate on any matter which he had to deal with. He had been advised to refrain from work until the headaches ceased, relaxation was to be his cure, thus George Battams remained at home and demanded that his wife look after him, at his beck and call. For a few months Mrs Battams did as she was told, but eventually the strain began to take its toll upon her health and she too fell ill, but her husband would allow her no respite. He was more ill than she and it was her duty to look after him! Battams almost had her a prisoner in her own home, his demands becoming more and more ludicrous. Eventually she decided that enough was enough and began to leave her husband at home and go out visiting friends. It was guaranteed that upon her return George would be argumentative and call her all kinds of names, but she could live with that; after all, she reasoned, she did have a life of her own and George was not incapable of looking after himself, was he?

The village of Heath and Reach where in 1882, the quiet existence of an aged couple exploded into violence.

On the night of Saturday, 5th May 1882, George Battams had a violent quarrel with his wife. He hit her and duly received a return smack. The couple quarrelled into the early hours before Mrs Battams retired to bed. George Battams found it difficult to forget that his own wife had hit him. Just who did she think she was? While George sat fretting downstairs, Mrs Battams sank into a deep sleep in the upstairs bedroom. It was to be her last argument with her husband, for as she lay there peacefully George Battams crept out of the house and fetched in an old billhook with a pointed end.

Silently, the old man climbed the stairs and opened the door to his wife's bedroom. Mrs Battams, unaware of the dark silhouette which stood above her, slept on. Suddenly Battams brought the billhook down upon her head, its pointed end cracking open her skull and spurting brain tissue over the pillow. Battams brought down the billhook one more time before returning down the stairs and sitting before the fire. It seemed like an eternity since his wife had gone to bed and indeed it was now Sunday, 6th May. The Sabbath, he had killed his wife on the Sabbath! Battams did not move from his chair until the following morning when a neighbour called round and asked to speak with Mrs Battams. George Battams told the neighbour that she was dead, he had killed her, and closed the door. The police were called and duly attended. George Battams confessed his crime but seemed totally unaware of what was going on around him.

At his trial on 6th July 1882 it was learned from other members of the Battams family that George Battams' brother had died in a lunatic asylum, and a further brother was now incarcerated as an imbecile at the Ampthill Union Workhouse in Bedford. His sister had attempted to commit suicide, and indeed she was successful, but not before she had suffered greatly, passing away some time after her attempt! The reason for her suicide attempt was believed to be that she was about to be taken to a lunatic asylum.

As George Battams stood in the dock at Bedford Assizes, it took no medical knowledge to diagnose that he too was mentally ill. He gave the appearance of daydreaming but every so often would scream out abuse, not directed towards anyone in particular as he had no perception as to where he was or the reasons behind it. This poor man was subsequently detained at Her Majesty's pleasure, on the grounds of insanity.

THE THREE UNWISE MEN
OF HERTFORD

WILLIAM Bennett had been a resident of Hertford almost all of his life. In 1837 he resided in a small cottage on the outskirts of the town and was known by most people who lived in the area. Bennett, who had served in the 49th Regiment of Foot, was an aged pensioner and of a pleasant disposition, his health was good and he had very little to concern him. He maintained a reasonable standard of fitness by taking a brisk daily walk through the villages surrounding Hertford and through the town, partaking of an occasional ale in one of the local hostelries. Bennett was a creature of habit, he rarely altered his timetable, drinking in the same inns, walking through the same villages at the same times each week.

Financially, Bennett was more than secure. He had saved money in his early years and now received a pension from the services of one shilling and tenpence halfpenny per day, which in 1837 was a reasonable sum, more than many other people in the town could hope to receive. The payment of these funds, as one can imagine, aroused the attention of the criminal class, and on more than one occasion he had been followed on his route by groups of men, who were undoubtedly awaiting the opportunity of robbing him once he collected his pension.

Bennett was too wise for such basic rogues. He would refrain from collecting his pension when he sensed danger and just to be on the safe side, he would not collect it for periods of up to three months, thus receiving it on a quarterly basis. Obviously, once every three months he was in a situation where he had a good deal of money on his person. This made him extremely vulnerable, but to get round this he would visit the police station in Hertford and get an officer to escort him through the town and ensure that he was not being followed.

Such was the situation in the genteel life of William Bennett, a man who had fought for his country and who now kept himself to himself.

On Wednesday, 28th October 1837, Bennett left his home early in the morning and commenced his travels around the town. It was his intention to collect his pension, but that was much later, closer to noon. Bennett strolled through the town visiting his usual haunts and passing the time of day with everyone he met. Eventually he made his way to the police station where he spoke with Superintendent Duncan, who duly offered to escort Bennett. Duncan observed that Bennett had other money about his person and warned him to keep it hidden in a safe place, rather than flaunt it about the town. The pensioner agreed, and collected the pension which was of an amount close to £10. It was close to four o'clock when Superintendent Duncan bid Bennett a safe journey home and escorted him out of the town centre.

At 4.15 that same afternoon a young boy by the name of Bolton met Bennett on his journey home. He stood and talked to the pensioner and while he was doing so he saw four men in a wooded copse close to the road near where they stood. Bolton pointed the men out to Bennett but he declared that he knew them well and that they did not bother him, and with that Bennett continued his journey.

It was 5.30 the following morning when a labourer walking along the road to Temen discovered the body of William Bennett. In utter shock he ran to Hertford and informed the police of his discovery. The body was removed from the roadside to The Feathers public house where it was examined by Mr Davies, the local surgeon. William Bennett had suffered greatly in his moments of death. His head was all but crushed and was almost unrecognisable; he had been battered and bludgeoned to death.

Superintendent Duncan searched through Bennett's clothing and found that most of his money was missing, as too were his gold watch and personal pocket book. Duncan informed the local magistrate of the crime, who instructed Duncan to carry out a detailed investigation in order that the unscrupulous villains might be detained.

Duncan detailed Constables Knight and Baker to assist with enquiries. The police were faced with the arduous task of speaking to everyone in the town in the hope that they might have noticed something unusual. It was not too long before the young Bolton boy came forward and told of the four men he had seen in the copse. This was confirmed by another traveller who had noticed the group, two of whom he recognised as a George Fletcher and a man named Sams. The information was passed on to the Superintendent who authorised the officers to arrest the pair, both of whom were well known to police.

Fletcher and Sams were duly arrested and taken to the lock-up where they were questioned about the crime. Sams confessed to the authorities that a further two men, William Roach and Thomas Taylor had been involved. It took a few days but William Roach was located in London by an alert officer who recognised him from the description passed from Hertford. Roach, realising that the police constable had recognised him, mingled with the crowds who lined the streets to celebrate Lord Mayor's Day, but not to be beaten the officer followed him and duly pulled him from the crowd and effected an arrest. No trace of Thomas Taylor could be found anywhere but the police were quite satisfied with three

Hertford as it would have looked when William Bennett took his daily walks. This view looks down Fore Street towards the Shire Hall, where Bennett's murderers were to be tried. (Hertford Museum)

out of the four. Taylor would surface again. His sort always did. Individually the three prisoners were brought before Mr Carter, the local magistrate and each made separate statements to him, all of which corroborated the details of the crime.

It seems that the men waited for Bennett to pass knowing full well that he carried money on his person. There were four of them, but Sams played no part in the actual attack. He had accompanied the men in the full knowledge that the robbery was going to take place, but as they approached Bennett he had panicked in case the old man recognised him and retreated back into the copse. The other three, Fletcher, Roach and Taylor crept up behind the old man and tripped him so that he fell to the ground. He was then leapt upon and beaten. He shouted out that he knew the identity of his assailants but this did little to prevent them from carrying out the robbery. Bennett's money and valuables were stolen and as he lay there the men continually kicked and beat him about the head. They then left the body where it was found and divided the booty between them. The men claimed that it was not their original intention to use any violence, it was a spur of the moment reaction. Taylor was implicated as the most prominent of the group and also the most violent!

The three prisoners were tried at the Hertford Assizes, before Mr Justice Vaughan, on Friday, 2nd March 1838. There was no doubt of their guilt, each of the three had all but confessed, apart from Sams, who was fortunate not to have played a greater role and by virtue of this was acquitted. Fletcher and Roach were found guilty and sentenced to death. Despite appeals and desperate cries for leniency there was to be no reprieve for the pair. It was commonly thought that it was a waste of two young lives, especially when the worst of the group, Taylor, was still at large and he was the one who had encouraged the group to carry out the crime, but quite correctly Mr Vaughan refused to alter his decision. Fletcher and Roach were executed at Hertford on Wednesday, 14th March 1838.

It was six months later when Thomas Taylor surfaced in Plymouth. He had joined the 15th Regiment of Foot almost immediately after the murder, using the name of Evans. He was recognised by the police, who carried out an investigation into his background and confirmed his real identity to be that of the man wanted by Hertford police. Taylor was conveyed to the town and found guilty at the subsequent trial. He was sentenced to death and this was carried out a few days later.

Avarice can be a dangerous thing, but it was the unnecessary brutality of the crime that caused the public in general to turn against the killers. Not one of the three who were executed could with truth attach more blame to the others, all were equally guilty.

MURDER
IN LUTON

CONVENIENTLY located today off the M1 motorway and the A6 trunk road, Luton has since Victorian times been a thriving business town. Running through the centre of the town is the river Lea and it is this which interests us most within the context of this tale of murder.

In the fresh afternoon temperature of a foggy November in 1943, two sewer men were ambling along the banks of the river Lea. Their task had been to measure water levels and neither man could be said to have been over-enthusiastic about their respective roles. Then the two men noticed a hessian sack roughly tied into a bundle which lay in about six inches of water in the Lea. They decided to investigate and received the fright of their lives when it suddenly dawned upon them that the sacking contained what appeared to be human remains.

Immediately, the police were called and within a short time of the discovery the area had been sealed off. Detective Inspector Thomas removed the sack from the cold dirty water and carefully unwrapped it upon the river bank. Contained within were the remains of a woman, naked and bound at her ankles and wrists, which were tied together. The unfortunate woman's face was so viciously battered that it seemed it was going to be an almost impossible task to identify her; her teeth had been removed and there were no rings or jewellery which might help. Inspector Finch of the

Luton CID consulted with Thomas and both men decided that the murder had taken place elsewhere and the remains dumped where they were discovered. Running alongside the river was a footpath which was regularly used by dozens of workers for the nearby Vauxhall plant. After a brief discussion it was decided to call in detectives from Scotland Yard.

Chief Inspector Bill ('Cherub') Chapman and Detective Sergeant William Judge were deployed to Bedfordshire. The initial task facing the detectives was that of identifying the woman. Doctor Keith Simpson was also requested to attend in order to examine the remains.

Simpson confirmed that death had come about by virtue of a heavy and violent blow to the victim's head, which had fractured her jaw and split her ear; the blow had caused a haemorrhage of the brain which killed her. Simpson painstakingly examined the whole of the body, which he estimated to belong to a woman aged approximately 30 to 35 years. It was confirmed that she had brown eyes and dark coloured hair which she had worn in a bobbed style, she had been five feet three inches tall and had borne at least one child and was at the time of her death, five months pregnant. Despite this welter of information supplied by Simpson there was still very little upon which the police could act. Inspector Finch had arranged for the woman's fingerprints to be taken after she had been examined at the Luton and Dunstable Hospital; these, like all other such prints, were submitted to the Central Criminal Records Office for comparison and, Finch hoped, would identify the corpse.

The body was photographed and the resulting pictures were to feature upon the pages of most of the local newspapers; a lantern slide was even shown throughout the town showing the victim's face and a request for anyone recognising it to contact the police. As a result of this publicity no less than 39 people were taken to the morgue in an attempt to identify the woman, but sadly the results of this operation proved negative.

A thorough search of the scene and the surrounding area was carried out. The sack in which the body had been wrapped had previously contained soda, sugar and potatoes; the wrapping in fact consisted of two individual sacks, one of which had clearly stamped upon it the initials MFD. Further checks into both sacks revealed that they were distributed by a local dealer in bulk, he could provide no records of where individual sacks had gone. Next a check of the string bound around the ankles and wrists was carried out; once again the police were thwarted in their efforts, the string was comparatively common and could be purchased or procured from a number of dealerships.

Inspector Finch had identified tyre tracks close to the scene. These were photographed and matched to a milk float, and further enquiries confirmed that this vehicle passed through the area on a daily basis. A plaster cast of the woman's jaw was made and shown to local dentists who might be able to recognise and match it with one of their patients. Slowly but surely, the police found that although they knew a lot of statistics about the dead woman they had not a single shred of evidence as to why she had been killed or even her true identity.

Bedfordshire officers visited such places as laundries, in order to determine whether or not any woman had failed to collect deposited washing; shops were checked to ascertain if a woman had withdrawn her ration card; hundreds of letters were received from overseas servicemen whose sweethearts had ceased writing to them, the obvious conclusion being that their lady friends were the victims – every letter had to be checked out, resulting in the individual servicemen being notified that their women friends were alive and well or otherwise. Such enquiries take time and naturally, in every murder investigation as each day goes by more and

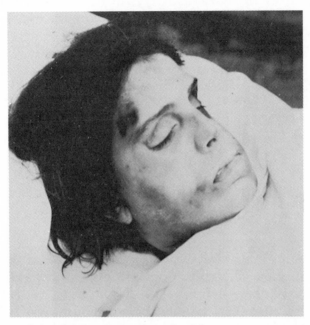

Pictures of the dead woman found in the river Lea in 1943 proved no help in tracing her identity. It was to be a stroke of luck that led detectives to the Manton house in Regent Street, Luton.

more evidence becomes lost, either by loss of public interest or by natural means. Lorry drivers who delivered to the Vauxhall factory at the estimated time of the murder were all interviewed; witnesses who came forward claiming to have heard screams and persons acting suspiciously had their statements recorded; dustbins and refuse dumps were searched for the woman's missing clothing. All of this was carried out with great expedience and thoroughness, yet all proved fruitless. The mood amongst those involved in the enquiry was less than optimistic.

The essential piece of good fortune and, one has to say, remarkable perception, transpired on 21st February 1944 when the Scotland Yard detectives in the area carrying out yet further enquiries noticed a small mongrel dog sniffing about on a small piece of wasteland. The dog retrieved a piece of black cloth, which it carried in its mouth. To most people this would seem irrelevant, but to Chapman it was of vital importance. He seized the piece of cloth and had it examined. It yielded a small label bearing the letter and numbers 'V 12247'. It appeared to be a cleaner's label, hence all such premises were again visited, though on this occasion a major breakthrough was about to occur. The label was traced back to Sketchley Dye Works in Wellington Street, Luton; it was the recorded number relating to a coat deposited by Mrs Caroline Manton of 14 Regent Street, Luton.

Records were checked and double checked. Enquiries had been made in Regent Street and the photograph of the dead woman had been shown to two young boys who answered the door of number 14. They had both failed to recognise the woman and the next door neighbour had similarly failed to identify her. Police revisited, and the neighbour explained that she had not seen Mrs Manton for a short time as she was away visiting her mother. Chapman visited number 14 along with Sergeant Judge. A young girl answered his knock, and Chapman was to later state that this youngster bore a direct likeness to the dead woman. He asked to speak to the girl's parents and she said that her mother was away in London but her father was home.

Within a short time Chapman and Judge were faced with Horace William 'Bertie' Manton, a National Fire Service lorry driver in the town. Manton, who had once been a boxer, seemed quite surprised by the police visit. He produced a number of letters from his wife posted in Hampstead, London and dated between December 1943 and February 1944. It had already been ascertained by Doctor Keith Simpson that the woman died on or around 18th

November 1943, hence the letters produced by Manton tended to point to Mrs Manton being alive. Manton further told the detectives that he and his wife had not been getting on, numerous quarrels had taken place disrupting the family environment and eventually his wife had agreed to visit her mother in order to let things calm down. Manton made a statement and agreed to allow the police to search the house in order to find a possible fingerprint which would eliminate his wife from the investigation. Manton seemed only too pleased to assist.

Superintendent Fred Cherrill, fingerprint expert of Scotland Yard, was called in. Cherrill was more than a little suspicious that no such print could be located in places where one would usually expect a housewife's print to be found, indeed hardly any prints were found within the main rooms of the house. Someone, it seemed, had gone to great lengths to destroy evidence of such prints. After hours of examination Cherrill eventually located a dusty old pickle jar in a cupboard beneath the stairs. He knew something within the household was wrong, every ornament, jar, even personal jewellery had been cleaned with an amazing amount of effort, ridding them of fingerprint traces. The pickle jar was seized and the accompanying print compared to those of the dead woman. It was a match and at last the dead woman could be given a name, that of Caroline Manton.

At Luton police station the police examined the letters delivered from Hampstead. It was noted that some of the letters contained a similar spelling error, the word Hampstead had been spelt minus the letter 'p', thus reading 'Hamstead'. Chapman asked Manton to write the word and sure enough he did so, missing the 'p' in the process. Manton's alibi began to crumble. He initially told police that his wife had decided to leave him on 25th November 1943, he had remembered this by virtue of the fact that it was the last day of a four-day leave spell he had been on. Checks were carried out revealing that Manton's leave had ended on 18th November 1943.

Bertie Manton had little option but to confess his crime. He admitted murdering his wife on the last day of his leave (18th November 1943), he further added that he had lost his temper with her after she had been seen in local public houses in the company of soldiers. In 1942 Caroline Manton had left her husband and gone to live with her parents, only to return four months later but the arguments and domestic disharmony continued until the afternoon of her death.

Manton's statement describes how he killed his wife in a moment of despair after she had thrown a hot cup of tea over him.

> 'I lost my temper and picked up a very heavy wooden stool which was near my feet under the table, and hit her about the head and face several times. She fell backwards towards the wall and then on to the floor. When I came to and got my senses back I saw what I had done. I saw she was dead and decided that I had to do something to keep her away from the children. I then undressed her and got four sacks out of the cellar, cut them open and tied her up in them. I then carried her down to the cellar and left her there. I went back upstairs and washed the blood up before the children came home for tea. I hid the blood-stained clothing in the corner near the copper.'

Manton further explained that he had made the children's tea and sat in the kitchen and eaten it with them in the full knowledge that his wife lay dead a few feet beneath him. After tea the children had gone out, providing him with the opportunity of getting rid of the corpse. After dark he brought her up from the cellar and placed her over the handlebars of his pedal cycle which he then wheeled to the river. Once there he laid her on the bank and simply rolled her into the murky river.

Manton was tried at the Bedford Assizes before Mr (later Lord) Justice Singleton. His counsel Mr Arthur Warde, KC attempted to advance a defence of manslaughter due to the extenuating circumstances under which Bertie Manton had lived for so long. Caroline Manton was portrayed as anything but a reasonable wife or mother, as the defence attempted to blacken her character and gloss over her husband's inadequacies. However, the case for the prosecution was led by the astute Mr Richard O'Sullivan, KC, who destroyed the mask behind which Manton was hiding. Doctor Keith Simpson had stated in his report upon Caroline Manton's injuries that there was evidence of her being gripped firmly around the throat by someone's right hand; her assailant had then pinned her to a wall or floor before striking her with a blunt instrument on the left side of her face between ear and chin. He was adamant that no struggle could have taken place after the blow to the head. In his second statement to the police during which Manton had described how he had killed her in a moment of despair and anguish, he had failed to mention gripping his wife by the throat. Sullivan managed to get him to confess to doing so during the altercation, not once but on two separate occasions. Bertie Manton was now being portrayed as a callous teller of untruths.

Further evidence related to small spots of blood being found within the house and detectives finding notepaper at the same address which matched the letters allegedly sent from Hampstead by Caroline Manton. Just to confirm matters, the piece of cloth found by the mongrel dog had been traced to a coat which Caroline Manton had dyed black in March 1943 in order to attend a funeral. Manton had thrown it away after he had murdered his wife.

Horace William 'Bertie' Manton was convicted of murder

and sentenced to death. This was later commuted to a sentence of life imprisonment; he died in Parkhurst Prison, Isle of Wight in 1947.

Bertie Manton was not an intelligent man, for such persons do not participate in such foolhardy activities, but one has to say he very nearly got away with the perfect murder. His misfortune had been his failure to totally rid the house and its contents of his wife's fingerprints. It was the tiniest scrap of evidence which led to his address, likewise the finding of the fingerprint, which tends to prove just how efficient investigating police officers are during such an operation. Certainly, Bertie Manton underestimated their professionalism.

THE MYSTERY
OF DEADMANS HILL

A FEW miles to the south of Bedford along the A6 lies Deadmans Hill, which lived up to its name in 1961, when what has become one of Britain's most debated crimes took place there. The lay-by on Deadmans Hill is today used as a peaceful picnic site, but in 1961 it was nothing more than a slip road of concrete foundation which was breaking up, allowing underlying gravel and dirt to spill out and cover its once smooth top surface. It was often used by courting couples, and ideally located for a secretive rendezvous as vehicle headlights passing along the A6 did not illuminate it, while on its western side it was sheltered by a wooded area.

Michael Gregston and Valerie Storie were two young lovers who both worked and had met at the Road Research Laboratory in Slough. Miss Storie was at the time unattached, a single woman with no commitments, but Michael Gregston was a married man with children. The relationship with Miss Storie had been on going for several months and Gregston had ensured that it was kept as discreet as possible. He certainly ensured that his assignations with the plain looking and somewhat naive 23 year old were kept at a reasonable distance from his home in Abbots Langley, near Watford.

On Tuesday, 22nd August 1961 Gregston and Storie visited the Old Station Inn, Taplow, Buckinghamshire. The couple left the premises at sometime around 8.15 – 8.30 pm, en route to a cornfield in Dorney Reach. They pulled into the field at about 8.45 pm. Their lovemaking was called to a sudden halt when there was a sharp tap on the driver's door window. Curiously, Gregston wound the window down. It was then that the barrel of a Smith and Weston .45 revolver was thrust into the vehicle, brandished by a man wearing a smartly cut, dark coloured suit and who spoke with a Cockney accent. The man said, 'This is a hold up, I am a desperate man, I have been on the run for four months. If you do as I tell you, you will be alright.' The man climbed into the back seat of the Morris Minor saloon via the rear passenger door and kept his revolver pointing to the front of the vehicle, occasionally altering his aim from Gregston to Storie.

Gregston was ordered to drive his car further into the field, which he did, and there the vehicle and occupants remained for about two hours. The couple's captor then decided that he wanted something to eat and told Gregston to drive. There followed a strange and obviously unplanned journey through North London suburbs. On two occasions Gregston was sent out of the vehicle, firstly to a milk vending machine, where he had no change to purchase any, then later at a garage for petrol. During this period the stranger with the gun constantly chatted about his life in prison; curiously, he could not pronounce 'th' correctly, he would pronounce this as 'f'. The journey continued north along the A6. It was now about 1.30 am and the man in the back of the car told Gregston and Storie that he wanted to stop for a 'kip'. Within moments they were pulling into the lay-by at the top of Deadmans Hill.

The car was stopped and the stranger brandishing the gun ordered Gregston to pass over a bag which he had noticed in the front passenger footwell by Valerie Storie's feet, but first he tied her wrists together using Gregston's tie as a

Policemen searching the A6 layby at Deadmans Hill in 1961. Today it is tree-lined and a popular stopping place.

restrainer. Gregston passed the bag over and as he did so, he was shot in the back of the head. Now the stranger's demeanour altered and he told Valerie Storie to climb into the back of the car alongside him. The terrified woman did as she was told, and she then suffered the horror of being raped whilst her dead lover sat motionless a few inches from her. The mental trauma must have been devastating. Eventually the man instructed her to pull Gregston's body from the car. This she did and pleaded with the man to leave her and go. As she sat close to the corpse of her lover, Valerie Storie must have thought all her nightmares had come at once, then suddenly from the dark came a further horror, for after asking her how to drive the car he fired several shots at the defenceless woman, who was struck in the legs. Slowly the man approached her as she lay feigning death beside the corpse of Gregston. She later remembered that the stranger had shiny shoes and wondered how and why he should have these when he had been on the run for four months. The man kicked Valerie Storie's feet and, believing her to be dead, returned to the car and drove off, crunching and grinding the gears as he did so.

At 6.45 am Valerie Storie's ordeal ended when she was found by a local farmworker. The police were called and within an hour of the discovery of the murder the scene had been cordoned off and detectives were commencing further enquiries. Valerie Storie was taken to Bedford General Hospital. She told the police that the man they wanted was aged about 30, five feet six inches tall, of medium build, with a pale face with deep set brown eyes and dark hair; he had an East End accent. Gregston's vehicle was located on the evening of 23rd August, parked behind Redbridge underground station in East London. Witnesses came forward claiming to have seen this vehicle speeding along Eastern Avenue at about 7 am, three and a half hours after the murder. Just 24 hours later the murder weapon was located hidden beneath the upstairs rear seat of a 36A London Transport bus along with five boxes of ammunition. Scotland Yard detectives who had been called in to assist Bedfordshire Police with enquiries were obviously pleased with the way matters were progressing. Several clues had been identified and more were to come. The owner of the Alexandria Court Hotel in Finsbury Park, London reported that a man by the name of Frederick Durrant had locked himself in his room for the five days since the murder; his curious actions had caused other guests to become somewhat suspicious of him. Durrant was interviewed and was identified as Peter Louis Alphon; he provided an alibi of having visited his mother in Streatham on the night of the murder, and he had later stayed at the Hotel Vienna, Maida Vale. Enquiries at this establishment confirmed Alphon's story.

August 31st saw dramatic developments in the case and

police enquiries. Valerie Storie, who had suffered spinal injuries which were to leave her paralysed from the waist down for the rest of her life, was moved from Bedford Hospital to Guy's in London. She again provided police with a description of her attacker and Gregston's killer, but amazingly the description had changed, the deep set brown eyes giving way to 'large, icy blue saucer-like eyes'. Elsewhere, Janet Gregston, who had visited her dead husband's lover in hospital, was in Swiss Cottage, London with her brother-in-law William Ewer when she suddenly grabbed hold of his arm and pointed to a man going into a nearby cleaners; she said that the man fitted the description of her husband's killer. Ewer claimed to have checked the man out and confirmed him to be a J Ryan. Ewer informed the police who ascertained that J Ryan had also sent flowers to a woman known as Mrs Mary Hanratty.

On 11th September of the same year the proprietor of the Vienna Hotel, Maida Vale contacted the police and informed them that he had found two cartridge cases in a room which had been used by a guest calling himself J Ryan on the night of the murder. Further to this the proprietor, a man by the name of William Nudds, told police that Ryan had asked him directions to the number 36 bus stop. Nudds was asked about another guest, Durrant, but informed the authorities that Durrant had remained in his room all evening on the night in question, and until around noon of the 23rd August. William Nudds had failed to tell the complete truth and certain enquiries made by police indicated that Nudds, who had a criminal background, had deliberately attempted to deceive them. On 21st September he was again visited by detectives who took him to Scotland Yard and asked him to recount events on the night of 21st August. He claimed that he had been mistaken in his first statement and that Durrant had been the occupier of the basement room (where the cartridges were later found) on the night of the murder. He further stated that Durrant had said that he returned to the hotel at 11 pm on the night of the murder when in fact he had not; Nudds and other staff were still up and about well after that time, during which Durrant had not returned.

The following day Peter Louis Alphon, 'Durrant', was named as the man police wanted in connection with Gregston's murder, resulting in Alphon giving himself up that same evening. Two days later Alphon was placed in an identity parade held at Guy's Hospital before Valerie Storie, but she failed to pick him out. The evidence against Alphon was fairly weak, the identity parade seemed to confirm his innocence and four days later he was released from police custody. Meanwhile William Nudds was again interviewed by police and now he retracted his second statement implicating Alphon/Durrant stating that it was all untrue, his first statement was correct. Thus the police turned their attention to James Ryan, which was an alias for 25 year old James Hanratty, an incompetent burglar.

Senior detectives fed the underworld information that the man they now wanted was Hanratty and it was not too long before the suspect contacted the press and police by telephone, refusing to give himself up as he was innocent. He could not provide an alibi for the night in question and believed he was also wanted in connection with other robberies in North London. Hanratty was eventually caught in a Blackpool cafe on 11th October 1961.

On 14th October he was taken to Stoke Mandeville hospital where Valerie Storie had been moved, and a further identity parade was held during which each man was asked to say, 'Be quiet, I am thinking'. Hanratty used the expression 'finking' and was at once identified by the invalid woman. He was then charged with the murder of Michael Gregston, his trial commencing at Bedford on 22nd January 1962.

The prime evidence of Hanratty's guilt stemmed from positive identification by one of the victims, Valerie Storie. Further evidence against Hanratty came from the most unlikely source, a supposed friend of the man in police custody. Charles France came forward and told police that Hanratty had once said to him that the back seat of a bus was a good place to hide things, hence the locating of the murder weapon became an important factor. Roy Langdale, a prison gossip and teller of many tales (most of which are irrefutably inaccurate), claimed that whilst a prison inmate alongside Hanratty, the latter had confessed the crime to him. Two other prisoners claimed that Langdale was a liar as Hanratty had always denied any part in the murder or rape.

Hanratty's alibi for the night in question was undoubtedly the chief factor in his subsequent failure to prove his innocence in a court of law. He claimed to have been in Liverpool on the afternoon of 22nd August having called into a sweet shop in Scotland Road and asked the way to Carleton or Tarleton. Police enquiries traced such a sweet shop and indeed the owner of the premises recalled a man fitting Hanratty's description asking those directions on either 21st or 22nd August 1961, she could not be certain of the date. The fact of the matter was that Hanratty could prove that he had been in London all day on 21st August, and if he could prove that he had been in Liverpool on the afternoon of 22nd August that would have left him with insufficient time to get to Dorney Reach and kidnap the young lovers.

Amazingly, during his trial Hanratty altered his alibi, claiming that he had not been to Liverpool but Rhyl. He said he had gone there to trace a man who was a 'fence'; arriving late at night, he further claimed to have stopped in a guest house close to the railway station, and he gave a description of the guest house, which had a green bath. A hired private

James Hanratty, executed at Bedford Prison on 4th April 1962. Doubts about his guilt continue to this day.

detective located such a guest house and the landlady Mrs Grace Jones confirmed that a man similar to Hanratty was there at the time in question. Mrs Jones was whisked to Bedford to give evidence in Hanratty's defence, but she proved to be of no help as the prosecution proved that every room was booked by other guests on the night in question and further implied that the books she kept in relation to the guest house were a shambles. What became lost, however, within the destruction of the Rhyl evidence was that on the night of 22nd August a spare bed which was in the attic alongside the green bath was in fact vacant, and the following evening (23rd August) a room in the guest house became available, therefore the possibility exists that

Hanratty *could* have stayed there.

The trial of James Hanratty lasted 21 days and at that time was the longest murder trial to be held in Britain. At 9.13 pm on the night of 17th February 1962 he was found guilty at Bedford Assizes and sentenced to death. An appeal was at once lodged with the Home Office but this was dismissed on 12th March, a petition bearing some 90,000 signatures failing to impress the authorities, and James Hanratty was hanged at Bedford on the morning of 4th April 1962.

The case against James Hanratty has never been accepted by a doubting public as being complete. In March 1962 Charles 'Dixie' France, the one-time so-called friend of Hanratty, had an article featured in the *Sunday Pictorial* which was titled, 'The Killer in My House'. A short time after the publication of this article France gassed himself, leaving a suicide note which read, 'They are going to crucify us all'. France did not allege Hanratty's guilt but declared his hatred for him for ever coming near the France family; no-one can ever truly know just what drove France to such desperate actions in an Acton doss house on 16th March 1962.

Matters were further muddied when Peter Alphon, or Durrant, began to make insinuations about his own guilt. During the years since the crime Alphon has confessed his guilt in private to reporters of the crime; in one instance he described in graphic detail how he had killed Gregston, raped Storie, then driven to Southend where he had handed over the murder weapon to Charles France, who had said he would dispose of it and arrange evidence which would frame someone else. Alphon further claimed that the gun had gone off by accident. Despite such claims in private, however, when confronted with the authorities he denied having made such comments or being guilty. Finally, in 1971 Alphon claimed that he would confess all in a press conference prior to the release of a book upon the case, yet once again he cancelled the arrangement and has not publicly commented upon the matter since. Is Alphon a publicity seeker or does he truly have a story to tell? More information relating to the case is constantly coming to light, including a link between one or two of the so-called 'innocent' witnesses involved in the case.

In 1968 the A6 Murder Committee was formed in an attempt to have the case file reopened; the main organisers were James Hanratty senior, Mary Hanratty, Jean Justice, Jeremy Fox, Lord Russell of Liverpool, journalist Paul Foot and Michael Fogarty-Waul. Some five books have been published upon the case, not one agrees with the conviction and all are united in their belief of Hanratty's innocence. Unfortunately it is the police who have faced the greatest criticism within this case, but the police simply act upon the evidence available at the time of their enquiries and one has to say that, albeit circumstantial, there was evidence which pointed to Hanratty's involvement in the murder of Michael Gregston, although many suspect that this evidence was planted and secured by the lies of several main witnesses, all of whom suddenly became law-abiding citizens when volunteering to give evidence against Hanratty. It seems certain that all has not yet been revealed in this case.

INDEX